MW00565349

Put Your Biscuits in the Oven and Your Buns in Bed

Nancy DeLong

Put Your Biscuits in the Oven and Your Buns in Bed

Written by Nancy DeLong
Designed by Jason Carey

First published in the United States of America by PublishAmerica, Inc. 2005
This revised edition published in 2016 by N. Glynn Publishing, LLC.
Lake Mary, Florida 32746

© 2005 Nancy DeLong
ISBN: 978-1-941320-12-9
Printed in the United States of America
Second Edition

N. GLYNN PUBLISHING, LLC

Website: nancydelong.com
Twitter: twitter.com/NancyDeLong
Facebook: facebook.com/ngdelong

To Jillian Reed Spires, my beautiful niece with a very kind heart, may this cookbook inspire you to become a five-star chef.

Contents

Foreword

The original concept for this cookbook was to collect recipes that taste delicious but take very little time to prepare. (More time to put your buns in bed, get it?!) It was originally thought to be for people who work outside the home and at the end of the day are tired, hungry, and cannot face another frozen pizza or TV dinner. It has evolved into a cookbook for everyone to enjoy!

The recipes collected for this cookbook have come from all over the country. Some are very, very old. Some are contemporary. Most of them have a story behind them—part of someone's growing up or family tradition. Or it may be a creative accident. Many are from my family. It's been my joy collecting them from relatives and friends, and sometimes that's the story. In fact, I've been collecting these recipes since the days when butter was a good thing, through when we were told butter was a bad thing, eat margarine with all its chemicals instead, to now, when butter is a good thing again.

We all have food in common. We have to eat to stay alive. Yet, more and more, I realize the huge emotional attachment we have to what we eat. It is one of our strongest ways to connect with one another. Sharing a meal with someone can be a spiritual experience. It's where memories are created. I recently took BLT & A (bacon, lettuce, tomato and avocado) sandwiches to share with my dear friend, Greta Hanley, and it was one of those unexpected precious moments that I will long remember. Meals shared with loved ones still warm my heart, from family holidays to specials dinners with friends, to impromptu "get togethers" with snack foods. My sister, Cat, for example, is a hostess whose presentation of foods always looks catered. And she and I can stand in the kitchen talking and sample every pot and bowl without missing a beat. (By the way, she's a slender size four, and I'm not, so guess who's doing the talking and who's doing the eating.) Both of my nieces, Jenny and Jill, have a real flare for cooking. They are creative and health conscious, so more of their recipes will be featured in forthcoming cookbooks.

Be spontaneous. I recently made a traditional Thanksgiving dinner for my family in March. It was a big hit, everyone ate and enjoyed it and kept saying, "This is so good and it isn't even Thanksgiving." Imagine that! Turkey dinner, as you will see in this cookbook, is one of the easiest meals to make. It brings family and friends together, and you always have great leftovers.

None of the recipes in this book have a calorie count, which will soon be passé anyway as we realize that the keys to proper eating include food combining, chewing, and drinking lots of water. And let me get honest right up front. Most of my own made-up recipes are estimated amounts because I tend to throw in the ingredients that sound good, taste it, and if needed, add a little more. So, I'll try to remember to put "est." where it applies. Likewise, if my adding and subtracting has ruined something, I'll share that too.

Some of these recipes are of the healthy variety and I have included a list of food combining and digestion times for things we all eat. However, that was not the concept for Put Your Biscuits in the Oven and Your Buns in Bed. I plan to do a sequel called The Wholier Than Thou Cookbook—No Sugar or Darnn Little.

I believe cooking is supposed to be fun and creative, a place where my imagination can play. Colors and how foods look on the plate are a big deal to me. And if I've included the recipe, then it's something I enjoy eating myself. I suppose that goes without saying, but I said it anyway. In honoring my original concept, many of these recipes are quick and easy. But if it takes time to prepare, then it's worth it, trust me.

The Original Biscuit Recipe

The original biscuit recipe for this book comes from Mildred Collins in Lexington, Kentucky. Her biscuits melt in your mouth. And because of Mildred, the first half of the title for this cookbook came into existence. Many years ago, I stayed at her horse farm and got to watch a little filly be born just as the sun rose one misty April morning. The filly was named April Dawn. I watched this little beauty struggle to get up and take her first steps, and then we went back to the house for a big breakfast, which included (you guessed it) biscuits and gravy. When I think of real authentic biscuits, I remember those beautiful mornings in Kentucky.

❁ ❁ ❁

Mildred's Homemade Biscuits

4 cups flour, sifted

3 Tbs shortening, chilled, regular Crisco®

½ tsp baking soda

1 heaping Tbs baking powder

¼ tsp salt

Buttermilk, cold and enough to moisten above ingredients

Preheat oven to 400 degrees. Cut shortening into flour and other dry ingredients, then add buttermilk. Mix thoroughly. Place on a floured surface and knead until you have the dough to a stage that is easy to roll.

Roll out dough and cut into biscuits with desirable size cutter. You can use a glass to shape the biscuits if you want. Place on lightly greased baking sheet. Bake at 400 degrees for approximately 10 minutes.

❀ ❀ ❀

Smile, it adds to your face value!

The Dessert Section

Yes, we begin with dessert. Be honest, how many times have you been in a great restaurant and you've said to yourself, I'll save room for dessert and you didn't? The solution seems simple enough: Do dessert first! And that's exactly what I decided to do.

❀ ❀ ❀

Mom's Pineapple Upside-Down Cake

Mom had a few very special things she made and pineapple upside-down cake was one of them. In fact, once she started making it, she made it all the time. She always put the cherries inside the pineapple circles, and then sprinkled the pecans around the outside. And she always made this in her cast iron skillet.

1 yellow cake mix, plus ingredients required on package (This will vary slightly from one cake mix to the other. Mom always used the juice from the pineapple circles for the liquid required.)

¼ cup unsalted butter

¾ cup brown sugar, firmly packed

1 (20 oz) can pineapple circles, drained and juice saved

½ cup chopped pecans

1 small jar maraschino cherries

Preheat oven to 350 degrees. Prepare the cake as directed and set aside. Melt the butter and add the brown sugar and stir well. Put this mixture in the bottom of the skillet. If you don't have a skillet, you're going to use two 9 inch round cake pans and pat the mixture evenly in the pans. You may need to make a little more butter and sugar and that's okay. Neatly place your pineapple slices in the mixture and decorate with the cherry in the middle. Sprinkle the pecans around the outer edges of the pineapple circles. Pour the cake mix over the pineapple, and bake for 45 to 55 minutes or until a toothpick comes out clean. When you take it out of the oven, run a knife around the edges. Let the cake cool for about 15 minutes, then turn it over onto your serving dish. It is best if served warm with homemade whipped cream or vanilla ice cream.

Love is a gift and a healer; it gives us the
grace that changes our lives forever.

Grandma Grace's Peach Cobbler

This recipe is from my Grandma Grace. She was the one grownup who always had time for me when I was really little. She would sit on the floor and play jacks with me, read to me, play Ginny dolls with me, and make my dolls fancy little dresses. She had a garden, a fruit orchard, and a chicken coop, where we would collect fresh eggs every day. She was a wonderful cook and baker, but when she died, I was too young to know the value of saving her recipes, so I only have a few of her treasures. This was one of my favorite desserts.

Topping:

1 cup flour

2 tsp baking powder

¼ tsp salt

1 stick unsalted butter, soft, not melted

¾ cup granulated sugar

2 eggs

6 Tbs whole milk (When Grandma made it there was only whole milk or cream, either will do.)

Filling:

6 cups fresh, ripe, juicy peaches, about 2½ lbs

¼ cup unsalted butter

½ to ¾ cups brown sugar

Just a hint of fresh ground nutmeg, about ⅛ tsp

Preheat oven to 400 degrees. Mix flour, baking soda and salt together and set aside. You're going to do the filling first. Melt brown sugar and butter together and spread the mixture evenly in a 9 x 13 inch glass cake pan. Peel and slice the peaches, add nutmeg, and toss lightly. Place this on top of the mixture.

Now for the topping. Beat butter and sugar together until light and fluffy. This is important; it will not turn out right if you rush this step. Add eggs, one at a time, and continue beating. Now, gently alternate folding the butter and sugar mixture and the milk into the flour mixture. When this is done, spread the batter over the peaches very carefully. Take an egg white and whip it, then brush it on top the batter. Sprinkle the top lightly with granulated sugar.

Bake at 400 degrees for 25 to 30 minutes. The top will be a beautiful golden brown..

Grandma Grace's Homemade Whipped Cream

1 pint whipping cream

1 to 2 Tbs powdered sugar

1 tsp pure vanilla

Whip together right before serving. You'll know went it's done because it will peak nicely. If you whip it too long you'll have butter. Now, serve the cobbler warm with lots of homemade whipped cream on top.

❀ ❀ ❀

A truly happy person enjoys the scenery on a detour.

Cousin Carole's Banana Napoleons

Cousin Carole has the entire cookie section. She is a fantastic cook. This is one of her super easy recipes and it is really delish. I use my homemade whipped cream on top.

1 puff pastry sheet from 17.3 oz box of two (Pepperidge Farms®)

7 or 8 bananas

1 cup warmed caramel sauce (Mrs. Richardson's® is a good one)

Preheat oven to 400 degrees. Unfold one sheet of pastry and cut into 12 equal rectangles. Place on an ungreased baking pan. Prick top all over with a fork. Bake for 12 minutes or until pastry is puffed and golden brown. Cool on the cookie pan over a wire rack or the sink. Cut each rectangle into two layers, which gives you 24 layers if you've done it right. Put one layer on each of 8 dessert plates. Slice the bananas in a bowl and add ½ cup of caramel sauce. Put a layer of this over the pastry on the plate then add another layer of bananas. Add a third piece of pastry and top with remaining bananas. Drizzle with caramel sauce.

❀ ❀ ❀

Love is allowing others to be perfectly themselves.

Grandma Nellie's Yellow Cake Bars

You'll hear lots about Grandma Nellie in this cookbook. She loved to shop and she made a fashion statement with purple hats and leopard coats long before they came into vogue. She loved to travel in the "Blue Goose," a remodeled school bus that was fixed up like a travel trailer. She loved to cook and she loved for people to enjoy eating what she cooked. (She was also known for leaving out an ingredient when sharing a recipe, so hers would always taste best. We can only hope all the ingredients are in this one.) Also, whatever she tasted you could count on her saying, "Humm" or "Simply delicious!"

> 1 box super moist yellow cake mix
>
> 1 stick unsalted butter
>
> 1 egg
>
> 1 cup finely chopped nuts
>
> 8 oz pkg cream cheese, softened
>
> 2 eggs
>
> 1 lb powdered sugar

Preheat oven to 350 degrees. Mix cake mix, butter, egg, and nuts together and press into a 9x13 inch buttered, glass baking dish so it is like a crust. Beat eggs slightly, set aside. Mix cream cheese and sugar together, add beaten eggs and mix until smooth. Now pour the mixture into your baking dish. Even it out. Sprinkle some additional nuts on top; it makes it real pretty. Bake at 350 degrees for 40 minutes. Yumm.

Faith is the bird that sings while the day is still dark.

Marie Harding's Yummy Cake

What can I say! This is another fabulous dessert cake. I made this for my sister, Cat's, birthday and my two nieces, Jen and Jill, helped me decorate it. Jen came up with a great idea. We iced the top of the cake, covered the top with a circular piece of waxed paper, and then we iced the waxed paper as well. We put fresh flowers on top, all different colors, and some on the serving dish. It was breathtakingly beautiful and fragrant. Then, when we were ready to serve dessert, we simply lifted off the waxed paper and there was our lovely iced cake.

- 3 cups flour
- 2 cups sugar
- 1 tsp baking soda
- ½ tsp salt
- 1 tsp ground cinnamon
- 1 cup chopped pecans
- 3 eggs, beaten
- 1 cup applesauce, homemade if possible
- 1 cup crushed pineapple, drained
- 1½ to 2 cups chopped bananas
- 1 cup vegetable oil
- 2 tsp pure vanilla

Preheat oven to 325 degrees. Grease three 9 inch cake pans with unsalted butter and cover with a layer of very fine, flavorless bread crumbs and set aside. Marie told me that the reason for this is regular flour will stick to the cake. I don't know; I just follow the directions. Sift together the flour, sugar, baking soda, salt, and cinnamon. Then add the pecans, mix through, and set aside.

This next part is all done by hand. I have an extra sturdy spatula that I got at the dollar store which works great. Combine the eggs and applesauce, mix together; add pineapple, mix together; add bananas, mix together; add vegetable oil and vanilla, mix together. Now fold the liquid mixture into the dry mixture a little at a time.

Divide the mixture into the three 9 inch, round cake pans. Bake for 25 to 30 minutes, until the middle of the cake is set.

> **Now for the icing:**
> 1 (8 oz) pkg cream cheese, softened
> ½ cup unsalted butter, softened
> 1½ lbs powdered sugar
> 1½ tsp pure vanilla extract

Beat cream cheese and butter together until creamy, then add the powdered sugar a little at a time, add vanilla, and when blended, the icing is done. Be sure the cakes have cooled before icing. Put the first layer on your serving dish and ice the top, add second layer, ice, add third layer, ice the top and sides.

I have also done this recipe in a 9x13 casserole dish. It turned out great, but it wasn't as beautiful as the layered cake.

❀ ❀ ❀

When you see the small miracles around you,
you will know in your heart that everything will be all right.

New York Sonia's Florida Key Lime Pie

Move over famous key lime pie makers; New York Sonia's here and has she ever blown your key lime pie recipes out of the water! Sonia Buonpane is a wonderful, outrageous gal, who knows how to make people feel welcome. She shared her version of key lime pie, and it is delicious.

> **8 oz sweetened, condensed milk**
>
> **6 oz evaporated milk**
>
> **4 egg yolks**
>
> **½ cup real key lime juice**
>
> **1 ready made graham cracker pie crust**
>
> **½ cup walnuts**
>
> **1 Tbs unsalted butter, melted**
>
> **1 Tbs brown sugar**

Preheat oven to 350 degrees. Combine milk, egg yolks, key lime juice, and blend until smooth. Set aside. Crushed walnut pie crust: Take fresh, shelled walnuts, crush them really, really, really fine, a food processor will work well. Add melted butter and brown sugar and mix well. Now take a ready made graham cracker crust and press the crushed walnut mixture into the pie crust.

Put key lime pie mixture into the crushed walnut pie crust. Bake in preheated 350 degree oven for 8 to 10 minutes. Let stand 10 minutes before refrigerating. Top with homemade whipped cream and lime slices before serving. Top with Grandma Grace's homemade whipped cream.

❀ ❀ ❀

Our words are seeds planted into other people's lives.

My Chocolate Rhapsody

This is one of my simplest and best recipes.

Carole's Chocolate Chip Cookies
Enough ice cream to make the dessert
Nutella®

Sometimes the very easiest combinations can turn out to be spectacular. That is definitely the case with this quick dessert. I keep Carole's Chocolate Chip Cookies (Recipe in the Cookie Section) in the freezer so I'm always prepared. This is a dessert you can make at the very last minute.

First, select beautiful goblets to use. Sometimes I mix them up if I'm having four to six people. Next, crumble enough cookies for the number of servings you're doing. Put crumbled up cookies in the bottom of the goblets, add your favorite ice cream (mine is Starbucks Java Chip), then drizzle some Nutella hazelnut chocolate on top. Repeat the layers several times. Top with extra Nutella, whipped cream and a cherry. Oh, it makes me drool just writing the recipe. It's the perfect chocolate fix.

❀ ❀ ❀

Dreaming is having the courage to follow your own star.

Mary Ellen's Chocolate Cake

Mary Ellen meets with her friends each month for conversation and of course, desserts. The group's Dessert Lady brought this one. There has been some debate about whether it is better in a Bundt pan. I made it in a 9x13 glass pan. It would also work as a two-layer cake. However, the Bundt pan was very pretty. It's rich, it's chocolate, it's delicious.

> 1 chocolate fudge cake mix, Duncan Hines® is best
>
> 2 large eggs
>
> 1 tsp almond extract
>
> 1 can cherry pie filling

Preheat oven to 350 degrees. Mix first three ingredients together with mixer, add pie filling and stir in by hand. Grease and flour Bundt pan, pour in mixture. Bake 40 minutes at 350 degrees.

> **For the Icing:**
>
> ⅓ cup milk
>
> 1 cup sugar
>
> 5 Tbs butter
>
> 1 cup chocolate chips
>
> 1 tsp vanilla

Bring first three ingredients to a boil on the stove for one minute stirring constantly. Remove and add last two. Stir until the chips melt. Drizzle over warm cake and let set. Refrigerate before serving. Great with coffee or vanilla ice cream.

❀ ❀ ❀

Chocolate was once used as currency.

Scotti's Cheer-Me-Up Cake

The sun shines for me when Scotti and I get together because she is a gracious, upbeat lady. She recently shared this recipe, which is a cake that needs no icing. For me, that's a big deal since I love icing. I sprinkle a little sifted powdered sugar on it anyway, just because.

> **1 pkg white cake mix, Duncan Hines® is best.**
>
> **1 cup vegetable oil**
>
> **4 eggs, slightly beaten**
>
> **1 tsp almond extract**
>
> **2 small boxes pistachio pudding**
>
> **1 cup of club soda**

Preheat oven to 325 degrees. Beat with hand mixer for two minutes only. Pour into greased Bundt pan and bake at 325 degrees for one hour.

When done, let cake cool for about 20 minutes and then turn it over onto your serving dish. Sift powdered sugar over the top of the cooled cake.

This is a perfect St. Patty's Day cake since it is bright green. It's easy, moist and delicious!

❀ ❀ ❀

Real kindness is given without hesitation
and without expectation.

Homemade Apple Pie

This is the real deal: Grandma Jane's Apple Pie. I was shopping with my sister, Cat, this past holiday season (2004) when I saw a couple fondling the apples. It was obvious from their careful selection of the apples that they knew something about making real apple pie. I introduced myself, and Mel and Sharon Borczynski, from New York, were generous enough to share this treasured family recipe. It's from Grandma Jane who was 89 years old at the time. She was a lifetime resident of the Buffalo, New York area. She had been married to Joe Borczynski for 67 years when he died in December of 2001. She has three sons, three granddaughters, and ten great-grandchildren. She still maintains the family residence in Cheektowaga, New York, just like she has since 1954. So I proudly share Grandma Jane's homemade apple pie recipe.

> **Two Crust Pie**
> **2 cups flour**
> **1 Tbs sugar**
> **½ Tbs salt**
> **¼ lb Crisco**
> **⅛ lb butter**
> **⅜ cup water**
> **1 tsp vinegar**
> **Plus a little water at the end, if necessary.**

Nan's Note: I know that Grandma Jane knows if it needs a little more water, but I don't know if I will know. I'm going to hope for the best here.

Preheat oven to 400. Combine flour, sugar, salt. Cut in shortening with a pastry blender. Add water and vinegar. Divide blended dough into two equal parts. Roll out on lightly floured surface to approximately ⅛ inch thickness. Line a 10 inch pie pan with pastry.

Nan's Note: If you are afraid to make this wonderful, delicious, flaky pie crust, then cheat and use ready made. Just know that it will not be as good as Grandma Jane's.

Filling:

8 to 10 medium-sized apples, pared and sliced thin (Grandma Jane likes Empires or Macs)

¾ cup sugar

2 tsp cinnamon

Dash of nutmeg

2 Tbs flour

2 egg whites

1 tsp sugar

Combine sugar, cinnamon, nutmeg and flour, mix with thoroughly apples. Fill pie crust with this apple mixture, dot with butter. Adjust top crust, crimp edge and cut in vents on top to the design of your choice. Whip egg whites and sugar together and brush top of the pie.

Bake at 400 degrees for 50 minutes or until done.

This is fantastic with vanilla ice cream or sharp cheddar cheese on top.

❀ ❀ ❀

Fear is overcome with action!

Fresh Fruit

Fresh fruit for dessert can be a spectacular and refreshing finale to your meal. But it must be a star in its own right. Otherwise, it becomes a collection of boring fruit chunks drowning in its own juice.

So, begin with fruit that is ripe and flavorful, which means in season. Take the time to cut the fruits attractively and uniformly. Think about your color combinations. Serve the fruit well chilled. Use the topping of your choice. Nutella is one of my favorites.

Do not add the topping until you're ready to serve your fruit because if you do, the topping will draw the juice out of the fruit and make your star limp.

❄ ❄ ❄

Knowledge is knowing that tomatoes are a fruit.
Wisdom is not putting them in your fruit salad.

Carol Peterson's So Easy Apple Crisp

This dessert will give you plenty of time to put your buns in bed!

- **1 can of apple pie filling**
- **1 tsp cinnamon**
- **1 spice cake mix or butter pecan if you can find it**
- **½ cup walnuts or pecans**
- **1 stick melted unsalted butter**

Pour pie filling and cinnamon in your baking pan. Mix nuts and cake mix together, pour over filling, and drizzle butter on top. Bake at 350 degrees for 45 minutes.

❀ ❀ ❀

Apples belong to the rose family as do pears and plums.

Tina's Baklava

It's very cool to have friends from different ethnic backgrounds. I was thrilled when Tina Lewis, of Greek heritage, offered to contribute her family's baklava recipe. Tina and her daughter, Kristin, share the family tradition of making baklava together every holiday. And I went to Tina's wedding a few weeks ago. She married a super guy. (Yes, there are still a few around.) So, Burt and Tina, enjoy putting your biscuits in the oven and your buns in bed!

> **1½ lbs chopped pecans**
>
> **1½ lbs. chopped almonds**
>
> **⅓ cup sugar**
>
> **1 tsp cinnamon**
>
> **½ tsp ground cloves**
>
> **½ tsp ground nutmeg**
>
> **1 lb filo pastry**
>
> **1 lb butter**
>
> **Small pastry brush (I got mine at the Dollar Store)**

Preheat oven to 375 degrees. Mix nuts with sugar, cinnamon, cloves, and nutmeg. Melt butter on the stove, removing salt scum which forms on top, until butter is clear. Brush bottom of 9x13 pan with melted butter and place one filo dough sheet in pan. Brush filo sheet with butter and continue this process until you have 6 filo sheets in the pan. Sprinkle the top filo with a layer of nut mixture. Add 6 more filo sheets, brushing each with butter and add another layer of nut mixture. Continue process until all nut mixture is used. Place remaining filo sheets over the last layer of nuts, brushing each with butter.

Cut into diamond shapes. Chilling for half an hour makes cutting easier. To cut diamond shapes, cut 1½ inch strips lengthwise, forming 5 strips. Cut diagonal lines approximately 2 inches apart, forming a diamond pattern.

Bake in 375 degree oven for 30 minutes. Reduce heat to 250 degrees and continue baking for one hour.

A note here: You will want to make the syrup ahead so it has time to cool.

Syrup:
2 cups sugar
1 cup water
Juice of half lemon
1 stick cinnamon
¼ cup of honey

In medium saucepan, bring all ingredients except honey to a boil and let simmer for about 20 minutes. Stir in honey and cool. Spoon cooled syrup over hot pastry. Makes 30-36 servings.

This is so good. Tina and Burt invited me over for Greek Easter dinner and she had made a tray of this delicious baklava. "Oh," I said, "let me take some for my sister and niece to try." "Sure," said Tina. Then I brought it home and ate it all myself.

❃ ❃ ❃

Life is not measured by the number of breaths we take, but rather, by the moments that take our breath away.

The Breakfast Section

Breakfast is one of my favorite meals and you can also have it for dinner. Breakfast is the one meal that you can not skip. I know you hear this over and over and it is absolutely true. If you're like a lot of us, you're still just grabbing a cup of coffee in the morning, or now, perhaps, designer coffee. Well, here's the scoop. Coffee, by itself, will cause your body to hold weight. I've heard this from medical doctors in health lectures; it's not just something I'm making up. What I do is have a piece of toast with peanut butter, or a small bowl of cereal if I'm not in the mood to make something. I will cook bacon ahead of time, only for a few days ahead, and then just zap it in the microwave and have it with toast and tomato. Another choice is fruit in a power shake. Also, I take a high- powered multi-vitamin in the morning, and if you write to me, I'll give you all the details about the one I believe works best. Really, we can eat anything that is appealing to us so long as we eat these foods in moderate amounts. Now for the good stuff!

Grandma Nellie's Buttermilk Pancakes

Dear Grandma Nellie made the best pancakes in the world for us. They were paper-thin and the syrup was cooked sugar. It has taken some doing to recreate the recipe since she did not write anything down and was rather sneaky about telling us everything that was in her recipes. Luckily, my mom left a written version of this family classic from my childhood.

> 1¼ cups buttermilk
>
> 1 egg lightly beaten
>
> 2 Tbs melted butter
>
> 1 Tbs sugar
>
> 1 cup flour
>
> 1 tsp baking soda
>
> ½ tsp salt

Mix dry ingredients together and set aside. Mix buttermilk, egg, and butter; add to dry ingredients and mix until the batter is smooth (no lumps).

Heat a little oil or lard in a cast iron skillet. Do not use olive oil or your pancakes will taste really weird. You'll know it's hot enough when you put in a few drops of the mixture and it cooks immediately. Pour pancake shapes into the skillet. When they bubble, it's time to turn them over. Just brown them, don't burn them. Remove from the skillet. Eat them hot, with warmed syrup and butter.

❀ ❀ ❀

Whole milk weighs more than cream, so use more cream.

Ever-Ready Bran Muffins

This recipe is from my friend, Joan Shinnick, in Lexington, Kentucky. She is a quick-witted gal who loves a good joke or can be a profound observer. She gave me this recipe when I first started this cookbook many years ago. I would drive back and forth from Ohio to Florida quite often, and I'd always stop at Joan's for a night. This would be our breakfast. Oh, and this is one of those recipes that you have to follow exactly or it turns out like crap, so don't get cute.

> 1 box (15 oz) Raisin Bran Flakes
>
> 5 cups all-purpose flour
>
> 3 cups sugar
>
> 5 tsp baking soda
>
> 2 tsp salt
>
> 4 large eggs, beaten
>
> 1 quart buttermilk
>
> 1 cup vegetable oil

Preheat oven to 400 degrees. Combine first five ingredients in a very large bowl. Make a well in the center of the mixture. Add the beaten eggs, buttermilk and oil. Stir just enough to moisten all the dry ingredients. Cover tightly and store in the fridge until ready to bake. When you're ready to bake a batch, DO NOT STIR, just spoon batter off the top into the greased muffin pans, filling ⅔ full.

Bake at 400 degrees for 12-15 minutes. You'll get a feel for when they're done. They will be brown on top and smell delicious because they are. This batter will keep in the fridge for up to six weeks, but I can't imagine it lasting that long.

❁ ❁ ❁

It's never too late to be what you might have been.

Cat's Breakfast Casserole

This is a perfect casserole to serve on Christmas morning because you make it ahead and refrigerate it overnight for the best flavor.

> 8 slices of white bread cubed
>
> ¼ cup chopped green pepper
>
> ½ cup spicy sausage
>
> ¼ cup butter
>
> 6 beaten eggs
>
> 3 oz evaporated milk, enough regular milk to make 3 cups
>
> 2 cups shredded sharp cheddar cheese
>
> Dash of cayenne, dry mustard and onion salt

Use cooking spray on a 9x13 baking dish and set aside. Fry sausage and toss in green pepper, drain. Toss with bread, dot with butter, mix together eggs, milk, and seasonings, pour over bread mixture. Put into baking dish, cover with foil, and refrigerate overnight. Remove from fridge at least 30 minutes before backing so casserole can reach room temperature. Bake at 325 degrees for 45 minutes or until knife comes out clean.

❁ ❁ ❁

The finer gifts of one's spirit emerges
in the presence of a believing heart.

Cousin Carole's Breakfast Casserole

This is great to make a day ahead and pop in the oven while everyone is taking their time waking up on the weekend.

12 oz of bacon or 12 oz mild or hot bulk sausage

10 eggs, lightly beaten

1 cup sour cream

1 Vidalia onion, chopped

1 green pepper, chopped

1 red pepper, chopped

16 oz mushrooms, sliced

2 cups shredded cheddar cheese

Preheat the oven to 350 degrees. Spray your 9x13 baking dish with cooking spray and set aside. Cook bacon or sausage. Drain grease and set aside to cool slightly. In a large bowl, mix meat, eggs, sour cream, onion, peppers, mushrooms, and cheese. Stir to mix. Pour into baking dish. (It's best if you make this the day before and refrigerate.) Be sure casserole is room temperature and bake at 350 degrees for 30 minutes or until golden color.

❀ ❀ ❀

Only two tools are really needed in life. If it doesn't move and should, use WD-40; if it moves and shouldn't, use duct tape.

The Big Deal Meal Section

I love Thanksgiving and I love all the traditional foods for this holiday. It's a time to get together with everyone you love and cook up a storm. And you'll have extra time to put your buns in bed. This section includes the famous turkey dinner, and the alternative, ham dinner.

The Turkey Dinner is the all-time easiest big deal meal ever if you have the right attitude. Consider a 24-pound bird for two. It takes about 12 hours to cook at low temperatures and that means there's plenty of time to put your buns in bed. I'm going to include the basics and some great variations, so enjoy. Or in the words of Grandma Nellie, "Eat and get fat."

The Actual Bird

I've tried about every turkey baking method over the years and the one that has always been successful and delicious is with the Reynolds Oven Bag. They have a turkey size for poultry up to 24 pounds. The bird is always very juicy, there's no basting, and it cooks in much less time.

Start by preheating your oven to 350 degrees. You must clean the thawed turkey really, really well inside and out. Be sure to remove all the innards from the neck and butt. (Be sure to do this step or your bird will taste weird.) Put the bird through three water washes to be sure to get all the crud out. I always salt down the inside cavity using sea salt, after it's cleaned. Dry the outside of the bird with a clean cloth or paper towel, tie the skin over the neck of the bird, fold the wings over the back of the bird, and tie the legs together. You can use string or thread, just be sure you remove it before you serve the bird. Set the bird aside.

Now, we're going to coat the inside of the oven bag. Open it and put in 1 to 2 tablespoons of flour. Hold the bag closed and shake it to coat the inside. Chop up several stalks of celery, a large onion, and a chopped up apple. Throw some of this in the bag and put the rest in the cavity of the bird. Then, very neatly, put the bag in your roasting pan. Now for the TLC. Make a mixture of a good, very virgin olive oil, a small amount of softened butter and kitchen bouquet. Now pour some into your hands and begin rubbing the outside of your turkey. You're giving it a rubdown, get the picture?

Then, sprinkle the bird with sea salt or kosher salt and pepper. Also, a secret ingredient here is Cavender's All Purpose Greek Seasoning. It's wonderful in lots of stuff. Before you put the bird in the bag, throw the following into the oven bag:

> **1 to 2 celery stalks, cut up**
>
> **1 medium onion, cut up**
>
> **1 apple, cut up.**

Close the bag with you hands and shake, shake, shake.

Okay, here's where you need two people!

Have someone hold the bag open while you gently place the bird in the bag and close it with the nylon tie. Then cut six half inch slots on the top of the bag. You can use a meat thermometer if you want, but I never do.

It takes about 4 hours to bake at 350 degrees to bake a 24 pound turkey. (Be sure to adjust your baking time depending on the size of your bird.) You can turn the oven down and keep the bird warm for another hour or two (love that buns in bed time). Be sure you take it out and let it rest for at least 30 minutes before someone carves it—oh please, I'm talking about the bird here.

❀ ❀ ❀

Gravy

I wish I could tell you something brilliant here, but I've never really mastered gravy making, so I usually find a tasty, pre-made turkey gravy and add it to the turkey drippings. I found a really good one called Personal Chef Golden Turkey Gravy in a bag at Sam's Club. It is 32 ounces of gravy, already made. I keep a bag in the freezer until I am ready to make my dinner. No one noticed that it was not "totally" homemade.

❀ ❀ ❀

"You can't blame gravity for falling in love."
Albert Einstein

Mashers

5 lbs potatoes
1 stick butter
2 Tbs sour cream
Half and Half as needed

You can double this recipe depending on the number of people you are having for dinner.

Do you like your mashed potatoes creamy, but not runny? I do, so this is how I make them. First, I use Idaho potatoes. I peel them, leaving a little of the skin on, then cut them into small pieces. I put them in a pot of cold, lightly salted water on the stove. When I have all the potatoes I want to make cut up, then I turn on the high heat and bring to a boil. Once it is boiling, I lower the heat so that the potatoes do not boil over. Do not over cook. It takes about 10-15 minutes, could be 20 minutes, depending on the size of the cut-up potatoes. I pierce with a fork and when tender, not mushy, I drain them immediately, saving some of the potato water. Then, return the potatoes to the cooking pan. Add about a half a stick of butter and a couple of tablespoons of sour cream, some half and half, salt and pepper. I whip with a hand mixer. As the potatoes become fluffy, I add more butter and sour cream to taste, then I put a gob of butter, a little salt, and a little pepper on top and put the lid back on. I do the potatoes so they will be done about the time we're ready to eat dinner.

❀ ❀ ❀

Quarrels would not last long if the fault
was only on one side.

Momma Reba's Oyster Dressing

This was a family tradition and people either love it or hate it. If oyster dressing doesn't sound appealing, you'll do just fine with a stove-top variety. Do it as directed and "doctor it up" with extra celery and onions, sautéed in butter. Also, you can make a perky dressing by cooking up some hot Italian sausage and adding it to the mixture before baking.

Mom made the best oyster dressing I've ever tasted. Other recipes I've seen have ingredients to disguise the oysters. She had a very simple philosophy about it: Oyster dressing should taste like oysters. Period. It was Dad's favorite dish. And now for the dressing.

7-8 cups stale, white bread cubes, with crusts (I like French bread)

1 pint fresh oysters in their own juice

¼ cup unsalted butter, melted

1 cup finely chopped celery

½ can low-sodium canned chicken broth, plus a little more if needed

2 eggs

6 oz half and half, plus extra because Mom said it should be moist

Pre-heat oven to 350 degrees. Butter a two-quart covered baking dish and set aside. Melt the rest of the butter (don't burn the butter) and sauté the celery for a minute or two.

Now, your bread cubes should be in a big bowl. Pour the butter and celery over them. Lightly toss. Add the eggs, one at a time, and blend together. Add the fresh oysters and their juice, toss; half and half, a little at a time, toss. Now the chicken broth, toss; your dressing should be really moist, not runny, but really moist. Add a little extra broth if needed. Pour dressing into the baking dish and cover. Bake for about 45 minutes covered. Then uncover. It should still be really moist and smell incredible. (If it's not moist enough, add just a little more chicken broth.)

Bake for another 20 to 30 minutes until the dressing is golden brown and bubbling on top. Let the casserole stand for at least 10 minutes before serving..

❃ ❃ ❃

With a bold heart, keep trying no matter what the world puts in front of you to handle.

Celery and Walnut Dressing

There's one other official dressing recipe I want to include. It's from a dear friend, and one of my first cooking mentors, Marie Harding. She and her husband, George, adopted me when I first moved to Detroit many, many years ago. They were Ohio State Buckeye fans, like me, so we stuck together on football Saturdays in Michigan and shared many wonderful meals together. This is Marie's dressing recipe:

3 quarts of stale bread cubes, a big salad bowl full

3 beaten eggs.

1 cup half and half

4 cups chicken broth, plus more if needed

½ cup butter

1 cup of chopped onion

1 cup fresh chopped parsley

1 Tbs salt

2 cups chopped celery

1⅓ cups chopped walnuts

½ cup chopped pimento

Sauté onions in butter for one minute. Add lots of chicken broth to moisten, toss together. Now this is where you really get into your cooking. Mix these ingredients together with your clean hands, squeezing them into each other. Turn into a buttered casserole dish, put a few pats of butter on top, and bake at 350 degrees in preheated oven for about an hour. Should be nicely browned on top.

❀ ❀ ❀

Women blink nearly twice as much as men.

Grandma Nellie's Noodles

2 cups flour
4 egg yolks
4 Tbs water
Pinch of salt

You will need two pots, one with boiling water, one with chicken or turkey broth. Beat egg yolks and water together for a few minutes. Add flour, enough to make a very stiff dough. Let rest 10 minutes. Divide into three balls. Put on a floured cutting board and roll very thin. Sprinkle with flour and loosely roll up like a jelly roll, starting with the short side. Cut to ¼ inch strips with a sharp knife. Unroll strips and lay on waxed or parchment paper to dry. Once all the noodles are dry, blanch in the hot boiling water. (Blanching means dip it in quickly, remove and drain.) This removes the excess flour which will make your noodles tough. Now, put the noodles in the broth and finish cooking. They will be tender and delicious.

Now that you have the basics, choose the side dishes that are the most appealing to you and your family. I've included some of my family's favorites.

❀ ❀ ❀

Love what you do or do something else!

Traditional Ohio Casserole

The state casserole of Ohio is this wonderful green bean casserole that has become a Thanksgiving standard side dish. You can safely take this casserole to any social event in Ohio and know that you will be accepted. (I'm allowed to say this because I was born in Columbus, Ohio.)

> 1 (10¾ oz) can Campbell's Cream of Mushroom Soup
>
> 2 (9 oz boxes) frozen cut green beans, thawed and drained (I like French cut) or 2 (14.5 oz) cans cut green beans, drained
>
> ¾ cups milk
>
> ⅛ tsp pepper
>
> 1⅓ cups (1 reg. can) original French's French Fried Onions

Preheat oven to 350 degrees. Mix all ingredients in a 1½ quart casserole dish, except ⅔ cup of French fried onions. Sprinkle rest of onions on top. If you open another can of French fried onions, add some more on top to cover it really well and snack on the rest.

Bake at 350 degrees or until the onions are golden brown, about 30 minutes.

❀ ❀ ❀

"There are only two ways to live your life.
One is as though nothing is a miracle.
The other is as though everything is a miracle."
Albert Einstein

Grandma Grace's Scalloped Corn

This is the first of several turkey dinner side dish recipes from Grandma Grace. And when she made this one, she had canned the corn herself.

 1 can (16 oz) cream-style corn
 1 cup saltine cracker crumbs
 ⅓ cup finely diced celery
 ½ cup finely diced onions
 ¾ cup grated cheddar cheese
 ½ tsp salt
 ¼ tsp paprika
 2 Tbs melted butter
 2 beaten eggs
 1 cup buttermilk
 Dabs of butter

Preheat the oven to 350 degrees, grease a casserole dish and set aside. Mix ingredients together and pour into baking dish. Put a few dabs of butter on top. Bake uncovered for 50 minutes. It will be nicely browned on top and so delish.

❀ ❀ ❀

*Happiness comes through doors
you didn't even know you left open.*

Traditional Sweet Potato Casserole

     3 cups cooked and mashed sweet potatoes

     1 cup sugar

     ⅓ cup butter

     2 eggs beaten

     1 tsp pure vanilla

     ½ cup milk

Preheat oven to 350 degrees. When using fresh sweet potatoes, be sure to wash, peel and cut off the woody portions. Cut the potatoes into quarters or eights, making the pieces all about the same size. Put them in the pot, bring the to a boil and cook about 20 minutes, or until the potatoes are tender, not mushy. Drain and mash with a little butter until smooth. Mix all ingredients and place in an 8x12 inch glass baking dish.

     Topping:

     1 cup brown sugar

     1 cup chopped nuts, walnuts or pecans

     1 cup coconut

     ⅓ cup butter

     ⅓ cup flour

Mix together and spread over sweet potatoes. Bake at 350 degrees for 30 to 35 minutes. This casserole assembled and baked the next day.

❀ ❀ ❀

Some pursue happiness; others create it.

Apple and Yam Casserole

8 yams or sweet potatoes (I honestly do not know the difference between the two, but I'm sure there is a difference.)

8 firm cooking apples

1 cup sugar

1 tsp salt

½ cup butter

½ cup cornstarch

2 cups boiling water

First, parboil—which means partially cook—the yams. Let them cool, peel, and cut them into large pieces. Next parboil the apples, cool, peel, remove cores, cut into pieces. Butter the casserole dish, place a layer of the yams, then apples, in the dish and continue to layer until all is used.

Mix sugar, cornstarch and salt in a saucepan, add boiling water and butter. Stir over medium heat until the mixture comes to a boil. Make sure the sugar is melted, let it bubble for a minute or two while you stir. Now, pour the sauce over the mixture. Bake at, YOU GUESSED IT, 350 degrees for one hour.

The nice thing about this dish is that it's not too sweet, but very tasty.

❀ ❀ ❀

A good listener is a person who can give you his full attention while he thinks about something more interesting.

Important Baking Tip

By now, you should have figured out that almost everything in this meal is baked at 350 degrees. I have no idea why this is, but it helps to be able to bake everything at once when you have several casseroles. Here's the tip, when you have more than one casserole in the oven at the same time you'll have to adjust the cooking times; it will probably take a little longer than is listed with the recipe.

If you want to make a salad, make a salad. If you want to serve bread or rolls, serve bread or rolls. You can do one casserole dish or several. At this point, you have everything you need to make that fabulous turkey dinner. And now for---drum roll please.

Desserts! Of course there must be dessert on the holidays. Not that anyone has room for it—it's just part of the tradition.

❀ ❀ ❀

A dog is the only creature in this world
who loves you more than he loves himself.

Pumpkin Pie

I promised to be honest, so here's what I do about pumpkin pie. I buy it at the store (the one's that are "homemade" by someone else) then I make Grandma Grace's homemade whipped cream which has already been included but here it is again so you don't have to flip back the pages to find it:

Grandma Grace's Homemade Whipped Cream

   1 pint whipping cream

   1 to 2 Tbs powdered sugar

   1 tsp pure vanilla

Whip together right before serving. You'll know went it's done because it will peak nicely. If you whip it too long you'll have butter. Now put lots on top of each piece of pie when you serve it.

❀ ❀ ❀

If we are here on earth to do good for others,
what are the others here for?

Grandma Grace's Sweet Potato Pound Cake

Grandma Grace was big on sweet potatoes, probably because it was one of the things she grew in her garden and stored in the fruit cellar in the basement, so she had a lot of them to use up during the year. In my opinion, regular cakes, with heavy frosting, are way too sweet for a holiday meal, so this pound cake is a refreshing change. It's a little more complicated than many of the recipes in this cookbook, but it is worth it.

3 cups all-purpose flour

2 tsp baking powder

½ tsp baking soda

1 tsp cinnamon

½ tsp fresh ground nutmeg

¼ tsp salt

1 cup unsalted butter, softened

2 cups sugar

2 cups cooked, mashed, and cooled sweet potatoes (2-3 medium)

1 tsp pure vanilla

4 eggs

Glaze:

1 cup sifted powdered sugar

3 to 5 tsp orange juice (fresh squeezed if possible) plus orange zest

Preheat oven to 350 degrees. Grease and flour a 10 inch tube pan and set aside. In a large mixing bowl, mix flour, baking powder, baking soda, cinnamon, nutmeg and salt. Set aside.

In another large mixing bowl, beat butter and sugar together until light and fluffy. Add sweet potato and vanilla and beat until blended. Add eggs, one at a time, and beat for 1 minute after adding each. Now, beating at low speed, add flour mixture to sweet potato mixture a little at a time until just combined.

Pour batter into prepared pan and bake at 350 degrees for 1 hour and 20 minutes, or until a wooden toothpick comes out clean. Cool for 20 minutes on a rack then turn cake over onto the serving dish.

Make the glaze in a small bowl, stirring together the sifted powdered sugar, and 1 tablespoon of orange juice at a time until the glaze is a consistency to drizzle over the warm cake. Garnish with orange zest. Cool cake completely and serve.

Tip: If you have pound cake left over, slice it and toast it for breakfast, add butter. Delicious.

❄ ❄ ❄

Ninety percent of what we communicate is not what we say,
but rather how we say it.

Pecan Pie

This pecan pie recipe from Grandma Nellie is the best I've ever tasted!

1½ cups Original Log Cabin® syrup
¼ cup (½ stick) unsalted butter
¼ cup sugar
1½ cups pecans
3 eggs, slightly beaten
1 tsp pure vanilla
Dash of salt

Preheat oven to 350 degrees. Mix eggs, vanilla, and salt, and set aside. Take a ready-made pie shell, place pecans neatly in the bottom and set aside.

Combine syrup, butter, and sugar in a sauce pan, bring to boil over low heat, about 5 minutes, then boil gently for a minute or two. Cool slightly before adding the rest of the ingredients. Add eggs, vanilla, and salt. Mix together and pour over the pecans. The pecans will rise to the top of the pie. Bake at 350 degrees for 35 to 40 minutes. Do not burn the pecans.

Another dessert to serve with real whipped cream on top. YUM!

❀ ❀ ❀

When I surrender to the wind, I can ride it!

Grandma Grace's Cranberries

Oh, one more thing for Thanksgiving Dinner is a cranberry dish.

Cranberries are not one of my favorite things, so if a cranberry dish was not a part of the holiday tradition I would not include one. But here is one that Grandma Grace served which is really good. And it's lots more interesting than opening a can that looks like cranberry Jell-O® and pouring it into a dish.

> 1 lb fresh cranberries
>
> ½ cup granulated sugar
>
> ½ cup light brown sugar
>
> 1 cup water
>
> 1 whole orange, leave peeling on, remove seeds, chopped fine
>
> ¼ tsp ground cloves
>
> ¼ tsp ground cinnamon
>
> ½ cup crushed pineapple, drained

Wash and drain cranberries and set aside. Bring sugar and water to a boil, then add cranberries, oranges and cloves, simmer over high heat, stirring frequently. Berries will pop open. When this happens, remove from heat and add pineapple and cinnamon, and blend well. Pour into container and chill in the refrigerator until ready to serve. It should be served cold in a pretty serving dish, the one you have put away for special occasions. This can be made ahead.

The harder you work, the luckier you get!

Thanksgiving Leftovers

Now for the wonderful world of leftovers. There are a bazillion ways to use your turkey, so I'm just going to include some of my personal favorites. You can make up your own and send them to me for the next cookbook. Fair enough?

Hot Turkey Sandwiches

Lay turkey on your favorite bread and cover with gravy. Zap in the microwave for about 1 minute. Eat and enjoy!

Cold Turkey Sandwiches

Lay turkey slices on your favorite bread. Add lettuce, tomato and mayo, also sweet pickles if you like. Add top slice of bread. Eat and enjoy!

❀ ❀ ❀

Growing old is inevitable, but growing up is optional.

Turkey Salad

2 cups turkey, cut in bite-size pieces

1 cup celery, chopped fine

½ cup carrot, chopped, for color

½ cup red pepper, chopped, optional

¼ to ½ cup bread and butter pickles, chopped

¼ to ½ cup chopped nuts (walnuts or pecans)

Mix ingredients together and make the dressing:

2 Tbs mayo

2 Tbs sour cream

Sprinkle of Original Hidden Valley Ranch® Mix

Toss with other ingredients. If you want more dressing, add a little more to the measurements. This is one recipe that you have to make suit your personal tastes. Add salt and pepper if needed. Serve on a bed of chopped lettuce with buttered toast points, which is a toasted piece of bread cut into triangles. Experiment and have fun with it.

Variations include adding raisins, orange pieces, sliced strawberries, or tomato pieces, to name a few (and not all of them at the same time).

Miracles happen, or is that just the way love is?

Turkey Tetrazzini

This is my version of turkey tetrazzini.

 8 oz spaghetti noodles

 4 cups leftover turkey

 1½ Tbs fresh parsley

 1 Tbs fresh rosemary

 1 Tbs olive oil

 1 Tbs garlic, maybe a little more

 3 green onions, chopped

 ½ lb sliced mushrooms, fresh are best

 1 cup low-sodium chicken broth

 2 Tbs unsalted butter, melted

 2 cans cream of mushroom soup

 1 Tbs flour, plus a little more if needed

 ½ cup milk

 2 egg yolks

 ½ cup Italian bread crumbs

 ½ cup grated Parmesan or Romano

Preheat oven to 350 degrees. Cook spaghetti as directed, drain, and set aside. Put turkey in a bowl, toss with the fresh parsley and rosemary, and set aside.

Now, put the olive oil in an iron skillet over medium heat, add garlic, onion and mushrooms and lightly brown. Pour it into a bowl and set aside. Look around. Do you have three bowls of stuff? Good.

Now heat the chicken broth and add the butter. Whisk in the flour, stirring out the lumps. Continue to cook this until the sauce is thick and smooth, about 5 minutes. Now add mushrooms and turkey. Blend together. Stir in milk and yolks. Cook until heated through. Do not boil. Remove from burner and fold in the cooked spaghetti.

Put mixture into a buttered 9x13 inch glass baking dish. Be sure it's juicy. Add a little chicken broth if needed. Mix bread crumbs and cheese together and sprinkle on top. Bake for 25 to 30 minutes. It will be bubbly and browned on top.

❀ ❀ ❀

Hearing tells us that the music is playing.
Listening tells us what the song is saying.

Nan's Turkey Soup

You've got this turkey carcass and you're saying to yourself, what do I do now? You boil it in a big pot, that's what you do. I add some fresh parsley, some fresh rosemary, chopped celery, chopped green onion, a little pepper and that special seasoning I mentioned earlier, Cavender's All Purpose Greek Seasoning. I bring it to a boil and then let it simmer for an hour or two. It smells wonderful. I cool it on the stove. I strain it to get out the bones and anything icky, add back in the good chunks of turkey, and add a couple of chicken bouillon cubes. I bring this back to a boil for a few minutes, then I put it in a container in the fridge for a day. I take it out and skim most of the fat off the top. If I still want turkey, I make the soup then; if not I put it into appropriate-sized freezer containers for the amounts I may want and freeze it until I'm ready for my turkey soup. Be sure to mark the date on the container so you know when it was made and frozen. I have lots of variations. Here are two really easy ones.

Turkey and Rice Soup

Bring turkey stock, with turkey pieces, to a boil and add brown rice. Bring it to boil again, lower heat and cover, cook until rice is done. Serve hot soup with a salad.

Turkey Noodle Soup

Bring turkey stock, with turkey piece, to a boil. Add a can of cream of celery, chicken, or mushroom soup. Then add egg noodles, bring it to a boil again, lower heat and cover. Cook until noodles are done. Serve hot, with a salad. This one is the fastest of the two because noodles cook faster.

❊ ❊ ❊

Only the pure in heart can make a good soup.

Turkey and Broccoli Alfredo

8 oz linguine or angel hair pasta

2 cups turkey

1 cup fresh broccoli florets

2 Tbs unsalted butter

1 can cream of mushroom soup

½ cup grated Parmesan or Romano cheese

½ cup milk

A little pepper

Cook pasta, drain and set aside. Cook broccoli florets, with a little water, for 3 minutes in microwave, drain, and add to pasta. Mix together lightly. Add remaining ingredients and heat through. You can also make this without the broccoli if you wish. Serve with a salad and extra cheese for the pasta.

❆ ❆ ❆

Some mistakes are too much fun to make only once.

Cat's Favorite Ham

My sister, Cat's, favorite family meal is ham dinner. Here are two of her favorite ways to make ham.

Buy a smoked ham butt, rinse it really well, set it in your roasting pan and pour Coke® Classic over it. Cover with foil and bake in a preheated 325 degree oven until done. (My version of this same recipe is to use an oven bag instead of covering it with foil. It minimizes the mess and keeps it extra moist.)

Another ham butt recipe is crazy easy and very delicious. Buy the ham. Boil it for one hour, then put it into a roasting pan and cover, bake in a preheated oven at 325 degrees. The amount of time is determined by the size of the ham. Now for the last 20 minutes, cover the ham with natural peach or apricot preserves. Finish baking uncovered until done.

Carole Pope's Ham Glaze

Here's an easy glaze for ham or any other pork roast which can be doubled for larger roasts.

> ½ cup orange juice
>
> 2 Tbs brown sugar
>
> 2 Tbs orange marmalade
>
> 1 Tbs regular white vinegar

Pour over ham or pork roast the last hour of baking.

❀ ❀ ❀

Give people more than they expect from you, and do it cheerfully.

Yummy Potatoes

This is one of Carol Peterson's recipes and it's a perfect complement to a ham dinner, so I'm repeating the recipe here.

2 lb bag Ore-Ida® Frozen Diced Hash Brown Potatoes, thawed

½ cup melted real butter, save some for the top

1 tsp salt

1 cup chopped onion

1 can cream of chicken soup

2 cups sharp shredded cheddar cheese

12-16 oz sour cream

Crushed corn flakes for the top

Preheat oven for 325 degrees. Mix all the ingredients together and put in a 9x13 baking pan. Cover with crushed corn flakes and drizzle melted butter on top.

Bake at 325 degrees for 1½ hours.

❀ ❀ ❀

Be tolerant of people who disagree with you—they're entitled to their own stupid opinions.

Pineapple Casserole

This one is different and so good; it's a refreshing change from most of the side dishes you may be used to making. I love this one!

> **3 eggs, beaten**
>
> **½ cup sugar**
>
> **2 Tbs flour**
>
> **1 large can crushed pineapple, drained**
>
> **1½ sticks real butter**
>
> **12 slices of bread, crust removed, cubed, and dried**

Let the bread sit out overnight and dry out before you make this dish.

Preheat oven to 350 degrees.

Put bread cubes in a large bowl, melt the butter and drizzle butter over the bread, fluff with a fork (or use your hand to mix it together, I do). Mix in the pineapple, sugar, eggs and flour. Turn into a 8x8 glass casserole dish and bake for 45 minutes. Watch the bottom, so it doesn't burn.

❊ ❊ ❊

Be a pineapple--stand tall, wear a crown,
and be sweet on the insde.

Slaw

Here's how I feel about slaw. It's a lot of work for homemade and there are many different ready-made ones available. Find the one that suits your taste, buy it, bring it home, put it in a fancy dish and pass it off as your own. It's one more of my little cooking secret, just sayin'.

Regular Baked Beans

Baked beans are an easy side dish. You can get the least expensive ones because you're going to "doctor them up" anyway. This is not a diet food dish, so when you make this, enjoy it. Fair enough?

Buy enough baked beans to serve the number of people you'll be feeding. Pour the beans into a casserole dish. Add chopped green onion, small pieces of uncooked bacon, brown sugar or maple syrup, ketchup, a little mustard and mix together. Put bacon slices on top. Bake in preheated oven at 350 degrees for about 1 hour, until bacon is crisp on top.

❀ ❀ ❀

Everyone seems normal until you get to know 'em.

Hamburger and Baked Beans Casserole

This is an interesting variation on an old standby. It can be a meal by itself with a salad and some really good bread.

> 1 lb ground beef
>
> 1 medium onion, chopped
>
> 1 tsp chopped garlic
>
> 1 (28 oz) can baked beans
>
> 1 (8 oz) can pineapple bits
>
> 1 Tbs brown sugar
>
> 1 Tbs ketchup
>
> ½ Tbs mustard
>
> Bacon slices

Brown the beef, onion, and garlic in a cast iron skillet, drain excess fat. Pour into your casserole dish and add remaining ingredients, mix well. Add extra ketchup and brown sugar to taste. Put bacon slices on top.

Bake at 350 degrees for 1 to 1½ hours.

❀ ❀ ❀

Ketchup was sold in the 1830's as medicine.

Corn Pudding

1 (8½ oz) box corn muffin mix

1 (7½ oz) can whole kernel corn, drained

1 (7½ oz) can creamed corn

1 cup sour cream

2 large eggs, beaten

½ cup melted, unsalted butter

½ cup grated cheddar cheese

Preheat oven to 350 degrees. Combine all the ingredients in a large mixing bowl, except the cheese. Pour into a slightly greased 9x13 inch baking dish. Bake for 35 minutes.

Remove from oven and sprinkle the cheese on top, bake for another 10 minutes. It's done when a toothpick comes out clean.

Cut into serving squares and serve warm.

❃ ❃ ❃

When you judge others, you define yourself.

Family Favorites Section

These are additional family recipes, and many of them could fit into other categories. I wanted to share them here because not only are they delicious, there are sweet memories attached to them. Some of them are from holidays, others are inventions that came about because we were out of the ingredients that were called for and threw something else in. I hope some of these will become your favorites, too.

Cat's Pumpkin Bread

1 (8 oz) pkg cream cheese, softened

¼ cup sugar

1 egg

1¾ cups flour

1½ cups sugar

1 tsp baking soda

1 tsp cinnamon

½ tsp salt

¼ tsp ground nutmeg

1 cup canned pumpkin

½ cup unsalted butter, melted

1 egg, beaten

⅓ cup water

Preheat oven to 350 degrees. Combine cream cheese, sugar, egg, and mix until well blended. Set aside. Combine flour, sugar, baking soda, cinnamon, salt and ground nutmeg. Add pumpkin, butter, egg and water, mixing together until moistened. Reserve 1½ cups of pumpkin batter. Pour remaining batter into two greased and floured 9x5 inch loaf pans. Pour cream cheese mixture over batter, top with remaining pumpkin batter. Cut through the batter with a butter knife several times to give it a swirled effect.

Bake at 350 degrees for 1 hour or until wooden toothpick comes out clean. Cool for 5 minutes before removing from the pan.

❀ ❀ ❀

Gold is the only metal that doesn't rust, even if it's buried in the ground for thousands of years.

Jenny's Scrumptious Spinach Soufflé

This is a recipe that I invented years ago because I've always loved spinach and my sister, Cat, improved it. Now, my niece, Jenny, has perfected it and we make it a lot. It's really an all occasion family standby, not just for the holidays. Jenny's three-year-old, my great-niece, Madison, decided that this casserole and steak are the only foods she will eat at the moment. (Of course, she makes exceptions when sugar is involved.) It's a great main course in the summer, served with bread and a salad. It's a delicious appetizer. We like it warm or cold. It's one of those foods that you can eat standing at the kitchen counter while you are talking with family and friends.

> **1 lb fresh spinach or 1 bag frozen spinach**
>
> **1 small to medium grated onion**
>
> **6 beaten eggs**
>
> **1 cup sour cream**
>
> **1 lb shredded mozzarella cheese** (I also add some freshly grated Parmesan or Romano cheese, but it is not necessary)
>
> **1 Tbs flour**
>
> **½ tsp nutmeg**
>
> **½ to 1 stick unsalted butter, in small chunks**
>
> **Salt and pepper to taste**

Preheat oven to 375 degrees.

Prepare spinach with grated onion. With fresh spinach, cut with scissors and clean really well to get the sand out. Blanch in boiling, salted water for 3 minutes, drain really well, and pat dry. Set aside. For frozen spinach, thaw and drain, pat dry, and add grated onion.

Mix remaining ingredients together really well. It will be a very fluffy mixture. Add the spinach and blend well. Turn into a greased casserole and sprinkle a little extra cheese and extra butter on top.

Bake at 375 degrees for 45 minutes to 1 hour, until nicely browned on top. Let stand about 10 minutes before cutting into squares. Serve warm.

This one is also good cold.

❦ ❦ ❦

When someone cares enough to love me
in my perfect imperfectness, he gives me back the
faith I was born with!

Leo's Ribs

My brother-in-law, Leo, is a terrific guy who has been a true brother to me over the years. He is quite the master chef when it comes to the backyard barbecue. More of his great recipes will be in the cookbook, Put Your Burgers on the Grill and Your Buns on the Beach, which features summer recipes. Here's one of our family favorites from his grilling repertoire.

2 racks of baby back ribs, or more depending upon how many people you are feeding.

Dry Rub:
1 Tbs Lawry's® seasoned salt
2 Tbs garlic powder
2 Tbs onion powder
2 Tbs chili powder
2 Tbs smoked paprika
2 Tbs brown sugar
1 Tbs black pepper
1 tsp dry mustard
1-2 Tbs of cayenne pepper

Barbecue sauce, home made or store bought

Mix all of the dry rub seasoning together in a bowl. Bring the ribs to room temperature and apply the rub generously to the ribs. Rub it into the meat. Really get into rubbing your meat. Let the ribs sit for at least one hour.

Preheat the oven to 275 degrees. Place the ribs on a foil-lined baking sheet. Cover each slab with heavy- duty aluminum foil and bake for two hours.

Open and slather the ribs with barbecue sauce. Seal in the foil. Grill for 20 minutes on each side.

When you take the ribs off the grill, leave them in the foil and put them in a cooler (without ice) with a tight fitting lid for at least 30 minutes. I would say an hour, but I don't think you can wait that long. This tenderizes the ribs and I'm not sure why. Serve with your favorite sides. And as Hot Dog Nellie would say, "Eat and get fat!"

❄ ❄ ❄

My food choices are like a roller coaster,
and I'm here to enjoy the ride.

Jill's Muffins

I have dedicated this book to my niece, Jillian. Years ago, she became interested in cooking and health, so she has created many healthy recipes with a flare. She is already helping me with a cookbook geared toward teenagers who want to eat healthy, tasty foods.

     1¾ cup sifted all-purpose flour

     ¼ cup sugar

     2½ tsp baking powder

     ¾ tsp salt

     1 egg, well beaten

     ¾ cup buttermilk

     ⅓ cup melted shortening

Preheat oven to 350 degrees. Sift flour, sugar, baking powder, and salt together in a bowl. Make a well in the center. Combine egg, buttermilk and melted shortening, then add all at once to the dry ingredients. Stir quickly until moistened. Fill greased muffin pans ⅔ full.

Bake in 350 degree oven about 25 minutes. Makes one dozen muffins.

❀ ❀ ❀

Love deeply and passionately. You might get hurt, but it's the only way to live life completely.

Noodle Parmesan

This is so easy it makes me laugh! Cook 8 oz of your favorite noodles or pasta and drain.

While hot, add:

¼ cup melted butter

1 cup whipping cream

¼ cup Parmesan or Romano cheese

Stir into noodles. If you want to make it fancy, sauté some sliced mushrooms and toss with the noodles. Sprinkle ¼ cup of Parmesan cheese on top and serve. You can serve this with a vegetable or a salad and call it a meal.

❀ ❀ ❀

Smile when you pick up the phone.
The caller will hear it in your voice.

Bacon! Bacon! Bacon!

Okay, I'll admit it. I love bacon. I know I'm not supposed to, but I love it, and I'll bet a lot of you do, too. So, on a hot summer day, one of my favorite meals is some version of the crisp bacon and fresh tomato sandwich with bread and butter pickles and potato chips. (If you are watching calories nix the chips.) Also, this is a good place for the mayo debate. There is a big difference in the flavor of real mayo and Miracle Whip. I believe this ends up being a matter of personal choice; however, for the record, I am a fan of real mayo and I do not care for the flavor of Miracle Whip in anything. That being said, there are so many varieties and combinations of the BLT sandwich that it is an endless source of creativity. Here are a few of my favorites.

BLT - The Original

The original is bacon, lettuce, and tomato.

> **Crisp bacon**
> **Fresh tomato**
> **Lettuce**
> **Real mayo**
> **Your favorite fresh, homemade bread or toast gredients**

BLT & A

This is the bacon, lettuce, tomato, and avocado.

Crisp bacon
Fresh tomato
Lettuce
Real mayo
Fresh avocado
Multi grain bread

BST

This is definitely one of my favorites because I love spinach.

Crisp bacon
Fresh spinach
Fresh tomato
Real mayo
Sourdough bread

BTC

This one is a warm sandwich variation of the classic BLT.

Crisp bacon
Fresh tomato
Your favorite cheese
Bread of your choice

Assemble your sandwich and broil or microwave until cheese melts. Serve this with a salad for a great meal.

❀ ❀ ❀

BLT & P

This is another variation of the classic BLT.

Crisp bacon
Fresh tomato
Lettuce
Sweet pickles
Bread of your choice

I like to serve this with potato chips.

BST Salad

I invented this recipe one day when I got especially hunger at brunch time. I went to the fridge and this is what I found:

4 strips crisp bacon

1 to 2 handfuls fresh spinach

2 slices fresh tomato

1 Tbs sour cream

1 oz crumbled Blue Cheese

No mayo

No bread

Take crisp bacon, lots of fresh spinach and a few slices fresh tomato. Throw into a salad bowl and chop up together. Mix sour cream with blue cheese and pour over the top of the salad. Just add pepper, it is going to be salty enough. Toss and enjoy.

Here's a Tip: Here's something that seems obvious but I'll say it anyway. Always make sure your ingredients are fresh. If they have been around too long in the cupboard, refrigerator, or freezer, they will have a funny taste. So toss 'em and use fresh.

Destiny is a living masterpiece created by one's soul.

Nut 'N Honey

This recipe is so easy and just too good to miss.

Put your favorite honey in a pot and bring it to a boil, throw in shelled walnut halves. Continue to boil about three minutes then put on a clean cutting board to cool. Okay, now you want to know amounts, right? Here's my best guess. About 1 cup of honey and 8 oz of walnuts. What you want is a candy consistency, that when it cools you can cut it into squares. Actually, this is pretty healthy. (No white sugar or flour. Get it?)

❀ ❀ ❀

Spinach Artichoke Dip

I've made lots of different dips, both hot and cold. I had several great recipes for this cookbook. But the truth is, I found the Gardens of Atlantis Spinach Artichoke Dip that can be served hot or cold. The first five ingredients are spinach, artichoke hearts, Asiago, Romano and Parmesan cheeses. It's wonderful and economical. So, my recommendation is buy this and pass it off as your very special homemade dip. You know, use a fancy serving dish and talk about Great Aunt Martha's secret ingredients. Remember, creative cooking is laced with embellishments!

❀ ❀ ❀

*"An invasion of armies can be resisted, but
not an idea whose time has come."*
Victor Hugo

Beets

Fresh beets are the best, definitely one of my most favorite vegetables. Get 'em right out of the garden and scrub off the dirt. If they are big, you want to cut them into smaller pieces. If they are small leave them whole or simply cut them in half.

You can boil them or roast them.

To boil them, drop 'em in a pot of water with a little bit of sea salt or kosher salt, turn it on high and bring 'em to a boil. Lower heat a little and cook until you can stick a fork in them. Drain. Eat warm or chill.

For roasting the beets, preheat the oven to 400 degrees. This takes a bit of time, an hour or more, for them to be completely cooked. Put them on a piece of tinfoil on a sheet pan or cast iron skillet, drizzle the wedges with olive oil, and sprinkle with a little salt and pepper. Check after an hour and roast a little more if need be.

When the beets are done, they are sweet and delicious. I eat them without any butter or vinegar, but you might want some.

There are so many delicious things you can do with beets. They are fantastic in a salad, especially with nuts and goat cheese. I like to use the raw or cooked.

❀ ❀ ❀

Giraffes have purple tongues.

Madison's Fish Sandwiches

There is one more family recipe that must be included. To understand the creative mind of three-year-old Madison Taylor Jump, I'll share a little story. She calls Cathy and Leo, "Ma" and "Pa," instead of Grandma and Grandpa. Recently, they were babysitting her at their home and Maddie had just learned to lock doors all by herself. She did not want to leave, so she ran into her Aunt Jill's bedroom, locked the door, and there was no key to unlock it. Cat knocked on the door and tried to coax Madison out of the room to no avail. "Open this door, Madison. Pa is really going to be mad," Cat said.

Then a tiny voice said, "Who is it?"

"It's Ma! You know it's Ma."

"Prove it, put your toes under the door and wiggle them," Madison said.

Now, here's the scary part, Cathy did, and Maddie got down on the floor to check out Cat's toes. Finally, Leo had to remove the door, and Ma and Pa found Madison hiding under the bed covers when they got in.

Madison's Fish Sandwiches were created one day when she and I were having snacks. She loves Pepperidge Farm Goldfish Crackers and we had cheese slices. She carefully broke the cheese into little squares and wrapped cheese on the top and bottom around a goldfish cracker—tada, a fish sandwich. "Mmm, I just love these!" Maddie said, with every bite.

Madison has a variation of this with a pretzel in the middle of two cheese squares, but then it's a pretzel sandwich, not a fish sandwich.

❀ ❀ ❀

Your life will respond to your outlook.

Favorite Friends Section

This section contains a variety of recipes as well, and some of my friends have their own section in this section.

Carol's Yummy Potatoes

Carol Peterson is a petite, upbeat gal. She has become a very close and dear friend, always there with an encouraging word. And such an elegant hostess! In fact, right now we're neighbors, so we even walk together at six in the morning. Or rather, she power walks and I run to keep up. Her recipes are usually quick, easy, and definitely delicious. Here are some of my favorites. This one is also in the Big Deal Meals section because it is so delish with ham.

2 lb bag Ore-Ida® Frozen Diced Hash Brown Potatoes, thawed

½ cup melted real butter, save some for the top

1 tsp salt

1 cup chopped onion

1 can cream of chicken soup

2 cups sharp shredded cheddar cheese

12-16 oz sour cream

Crushed corn flakes for the top

Preheat oven for 325 degrees. Mix all the ingredients together and put in a 9x13 baking pan. Cover with crushed corn flakes and drizzle melted butter on top.

Bake at 325 degrees for 1½ hours.

❀ ❀ ❀

*A happy life is about seeing the blessings
wherever they occur.*

Carol's Broccoli Salad

This is one of those outstanding summer holiday recipes. It's perfect with anything made on the grill or down home fried chicken. It's one of my Fourth of July standards.

One bunch fresh broccoli

½ cup sunflower seeds

½ cup of raisins (regular or white or a mix of both)

½ pound bacon, fried crisp and crumbled

½ cup of green or purple onions

½ cup water chestnuts

1 cup real mayo

½ cup sugar

2 Tbs vinegar

Combine broccoli florets, sunflower seeds, raisins, bacon and onion in a bowl. Mix together mayo, sugar and vinegar in a small bowl, then add to broccoli mixture. Chill and serve. Best if chilled for at least four hours or overnight.

❄ ❄ ❄

The Constitution of the United States and the Declaration of Independence were written on parchment; however, some working drafts of the documents were composed on hemp (marijuana) paper which was widely used in those days.

Carol's Dill Bread in a Bundt Pan

3 cans of refrigerated biscuits, cut up into chunks

1 stick melted real butter

1½ tsp garlic salt

2 tsp dill

Preheat oven to 350 degrees.

Layer bottom of pan with cut-up biscuits. Pour part of the butter and seasonings over biscuits. Add another layer. Pour rest of mixture over the biscuits. Bake at 350 degrees for 22 minutes.

❀ ❀ ❀

You only get to keep what you give away.

Babz' Brilliant Fish

Remember in the beginning when I said if it's a longer recipe, and/or takes longer to prepare, it's definitely worth it. Well, this is one of those. Babz is a fabulous gal and a true gourmet. She explained that she invented this colorful recipe on the day clocks returned to standard time, "fall back day." It was also the day that her nine-year-old son scored the winning extra point at his football game and on top of that, Babz bought pumpkins that day, too. She was such a busy girl that day. She assures me that she will make this recipe every year on this very day as a new family tradition. Yes, creative cooks can be eccentric. I think it's a good trait, because then no one can say we are boring. For a thrill, just read this recipe. I'll bet your mouth will water. Mine did.

1 lb fish cut into bite-size chunks, choose a fish that is firm such as grouper (you may also use chicken, shrimp and/or scallops, but then the name won't fit.)

2 Tbs butter

2 Tbs olive oil (for step 1)

1 Tbs olive oil (for step 2)

¼-½ cup flour

2 large red peppers, halved, de-stemmed and de-seeded

1 cup heavy whipping cream

1 cup chicken stock or bouillon

3 cloves garlic, minced

½ small onion, finely chopped

salt and pepper to taste

garlic salt and lemon pepper to taste

2 cups pasta, campanelle or fusilli

6 cups water, add salt or 2 chicken bouillon cubes

Capers, lemon wedges, and parsley

Preheat oven to 400 degrees.

Place red peppers flesh side down on lightly oiled aluminum foil. Roast until the skin turns bubbly and black. Remove from oven and place in paper bag for 5 minutes. Remove skin and discard. Cut fleshy portion into pieces and puree with chicken broth in food processor or blender until completely smooth. Place in a large bowl and mix in cream.

Heat 2 tablespoons of olive oil in frying pan over medium heat. Dip the fish chunks in butter and lightly coat with flour. Gently turn the fish with tongs and fry on all sides until golden brown. Place on plate with paper towel. Do not cover the fish.

Heat 1 Tablespoon olive oil in same pan and sauté onions over medium heat until transparent, approximately 8 minutes. Add garlic at last minute to avoid burning.

Meanwhile, boil 6 cups water in large pot and add salt or bouillon. Add pasta and cook to desired tenderness. (Bite it to see when it's done if you can't tell by looking at it.)

Add fish and red pepper sauce to sautéed onions/garlic. Gently stir, add salt and pepper, garlic salt and lemon pepper to taste. Drain pasta, place on plates and top with fish and sauce. Garnish with capers, lemon wedge, and parsley. Enjoy the brilliant color and taste!

❀ ❀ ❀

Most lipstick contains fish scales (eeww).

Grits Casserole

As you know, I live in Florida now, so this cookbook would be incomplete without at least one recipe for grits. Here is a wonderful one from Mildred Collins, who shared her biscuit recipe in the beginning.

> **1 cup quick grits**
>
> **4 cups boiling water**
>
> **1 tsp salt**
>
> **½ stick butter**
>
> **1 (6 oz) cheese roll, garlic or sharp**
>
> **2 eggs**
>
> **Milk**

Make grits in boiling water, add rest of ingredients and stir until melted together. Then beat 2 eggs in a measuring cup and fill rest of cup with milk. Stir into mixture. Put into a buttered casserole dish and bake at 350 degrees for 45 minutes.

❄ ❄ ❄

*Advice is what we ask for when we already know
the answer and wish we didn't.*

Johanna's Broccoli Cheese Bread

Johanna brought this bread to a get-together I attended and I just had to have the recipe. First, I lost the recipe and tried to remember it and added cream of mushroom soup, which was a terrible mistake. Then I lost the recipe and forgot the onion. So at last, this is the recipe, easy to make and very, very good as an appetizer, with soups or as a main course.

> 1 pkg Jiffy® buttermilk biscuit mix
>
> 3 eggs, slightly beaten
>
> 1 small chopped onion
>
> 1 stick melted butter
>
> 6 oz cottage cheese
>
> 1 (10 oz) pkg frozen broccoli, thawed and drained really well.
>
> 1 cup shredded, sharp cheddar cheese (I use a little more)

Preheat oven to 350 degrees.

Use a 9x13 baking dish, spray with cooking spray, then flour your baking dish. Mix all the ingredients together in the baking dish and spread evenly. I sprinkle a little shredded cheese on top. Bake at 350 degrees for 35 to 45 minutes. Cut into squares and serve.

❀ ❀ ❀

Love can open any door!

Midge Norris' Best Friend's Grandma's Cherry Pudding

Midge Norris recently turned 85 years young. She is a delightful lady and I'm thrilled that she shared this recipe with me. She chuckled, "My best friend's grandma used to make this pudding for us when we were little so you can imagine how old the recipe is!" What a treasure to include this recipe from the 1800s.

2 cups sugar

Butter the size of 2 walnuts, unsalted (Remember, they didn't have sticks of butter back then)

2 eggs

2 cups flour

2 tsp baking soda

Dash of salt

2 cans of pie cherries, not pie filling, drained, set liquid aside. (Of course, Grandma made her own from fresh cherries)

1 cup chopped pecans

1 tsp pure vanilla

Mix the sugar, butter and eggs together, then add the flour, baking soda and salt, mix well, add the remaining ingredients. Again mix together well. Now, pour into greased 9x13 glass baking dish, bake in preheated 350 degree oven for 35 minutes.

Sauce:

1 cup sugar

1 cup of cherry juice, add water if needed to equal 1 cup

2 Tbs of flour

2 Tbs of butter

Cook over medium heat until slightly thickened. Serve it warm over pudding and top with homemade whipped cream.

Only you have the power to unveil the light within yourself and share it with the world.

Marie Harding's Leg of Lamb

Marie Harding adopted me when I moved to Detroit as a reporter for the Detroit News. I spent many evenings and football Saturdays with Mari-a (my nickname for her) and her husband, George. She and George were Buckeyes, and we proudly flew our Ohio State University flag in Michigan on those autumn Saturdays. And Marie did cook up a storm. Some of her prize-winning desserts are in the dessert section. She taught me a lot about making foods tasty and fun. She was always happy and laughing, and she always made me feel special and welcome.

Marie's version of leg of lamb is outstanding. Put leg of lamb in roasting pan. Rub leg with real garlic cloves, chopped fine, Lawry's seasoned salt, Jane's Crazy Mixed-Up salt, smother with chopped onions. Be sure to add a little water to bottom of pan.

Bake at 475 degrees for 20 minutes, reduce heat to 325 degrees and bake for 30 minutes. Cover and continue to bake until done the way you like it, based on weight of the leg.

❀ ❀ ❀

"The odds of going to the store for a loaf of bread and coming out with only a loaf of bread are three billion to one."
Erma Bombeck

Marie's Chicken Salad

1½ cups cubed, cooked chicken

1 cup celery

2 Tbs green peppers

½ cup grated carrots

½ cup chopped cashews

2 hard-cooked eggs

½ tsp salt

⅛ tsp pepper

¾ cup mayonnaise

Combine all the ingredients together, cover and refrigerate. Drizzle French dressing on top when served.

❀ ❀ ❀

Did you know that butterflies taste with their feet?

Marie's Spiced Peach Salad

1 large pkg peach Jell-O®

1 large can (2½ lb) sliced peaches (or fresh if possible)

¼ cup sugar

¼ cup vinegar

½ tsp cinnamon

½ tsp cloves

Drain syrup from peaches and save. Then, add sugar and spices to the Jell-O®. Add 1½ cups boiling water and stir until Jell-O® is dissolved. Add enough liquid to peach syrup to make 1½ cups and add to the Jell-O® mixture. Cool until syrupy and add the sliced peaches. Pour into Jell-O® mold and put in fridge to set. Serve with real whipped cream.

❀ ❀ ❀

Someday, health nuts are going to feel really stupid lying in the hospital dying of nothing.

Marie's Hot Potatoes

5 medium potatoes, cooked and cubed

¼ lb shredded sharp cheddar cheese

¼ tsp mustard

½ tsp mayo

Olives with pimento

5 strips raw bacon

Paprika

Salt and pepper the potatoes and add cheese, stir in mustard and mayo. Spoon into baking dish. Top with sliced olives and strips of raw bacon. Sprinkle with paprika. Bake at 350 degrees for 30 minutes.

❁ ❁ ❁

A best friend will always bring out the best in you.

Marie's Chicken Casserole

3 cups chicken, cooked and cubed

½ cup real mayo

1 cup Pepperidge Farm® bread stuffing

1 can cream of mushroom soup

½ cup milk

½ lb mushrooms

1 can water chestnuts, drained and sliced

Preheat oven to 350 degrees. Put stuffing in buttered 9x13 inch glass baking dish. Sauté mushrooms in butter, add remaining ingredients and mix together. Pour over the dressing. Bake for 40 minutes.

❀ ❀ ❀

*Discernment is a gift our souls give us so that
we can open our hearts to love.*

The Cheesie Biscuits

This one comes from Debbie Cody, a friend from Michigan. Get a box of Bisquick®. Use the recipe for biscuits from the Bisquick® box, then add about a cup of sharp cheddar cheese to the batter. Bake as directed on the box.

Melt ½ stick real butter with garlic powder to taste. Drizzle over hot biscuits. YUM!!!

❀ ❀ ❀

*Some mornings it barely seems worthwhile
to gnaw through the restraining straps.*

Super Salads Section

These days, almost everyone eats salads as a meal. So, if I'm going to have a salad as a meal, it better be memorable, not boring. Therefore, this is a very small section. My promise to you is that these are fabulous salads. You'll be glad I included them!

The Greatest Spinach Salad

1 lb fresh spinach

½ lb mushrooms, sliced

3 hard-cooked eggs, sliced

1 cup dried cherries

1½ cups chopped red apple

6 slices center cut bacon, cooked and crumbled

Wash spinach and pull off stems. Dry well and tear into bite-size pieces. Arrange in bowl with mushrooms, eggs, cherries, apple and bacon.

Hot Bacon Dressing:

½ cup sunflower oil

3 Tbs bacon fat

¼ cup ketchup

¼ cup cider vinegar

1 Tbs Worcestershire sauce

2 Tbs sugar

½ med. onion, grated fine

Combine ingredients in a cast iron skillet, heat through but do not boil, then simmer for about 5 minutes. Pour hot dressing over salad. Toss and serve at once.

*Friends are angels who lift us to our feet
when our wings have forgotten how to fly.*

Everything but the Kitchen Sink Salad

Sherrie Hill is a dear and special friend, very creative, and a lot of fun. And that's a pretty amazing combination of traits. Her meals are always deliciously memorable. Here are a few of her favorite salads. These are yummy and fun and creative and beautiful to serve. They are so good, they make you feel like you're not eating healthy, but you are.

> 1 head red leaf lettuce
>
> 1 can hearts of palm
>
> 1 can artichoke hearts
>
> 1 cup crumble bacon (center cut)
>
> 1 cup crumbled blue cheese
>
> 1 cup blue cheese dressing

Tear lettuce into small pieces and put into large salad bowl. Drain hearts of palm and slice into small circles. Drain artichoke hearts and cut into quarters. Add both to lettuce. Fry bacon until very crisp and drain off oil. Let bacon cool on paper towel, then crumble and add to lettuce. Sprinkle blue cheese over ingredients in bowl. Toss lightly with dressing and serve immediately.

> **Blue Cheese Dressing**
>
> ¾ cup mayonnaise
>
> ¼ cup sour cream
>
> 2 Tbs buttermilk
>
> 1 cup crumbled blue cheese
>
> 1 tsp Worcestershire
>
> **Fresh ground black pepper**

Place the mayonnaise, sour cream, buttermilk, and Worcestershire, to taste, in the bowl of a food processor or blender. Process until very smooth. Scrape the mixture into a small bowl. Fold in blue cheese. Allow to stand at room temperature for 30 minutes before using as salad dressing.

❀ ❀ ❀

Make peace with your past so it doesn't ruin your present.

Honey Lime Chicken Salad

1 head romaine lettuce

4 boneless skinless chicken breasts, broiled

1 cup toasted slivered almonds

1 cup chopped celery

Fresh ground black pepper

Cut bottom off of romaine lettuce. Keep leaves whole and fan individual leaves on plates (about 5 per plate). Cut broiled chicken breasts into bite-size pieces and put in mixing bowl. Put slivered almonds in a single layer on a cookie sheet and toast under broiler until golden—watch carefully! Add toasted almonds and celery to chicken. Add dressing and toss. Scoop out chicken mixture with large ice cream scoop onto beds of lettuce. Garnish with lime wedges. Sprinkle with fresh ground black pepper and serve.

Honey Lime Dressing

1 (8 oz) pkg cream cheese

2 Tbs mayonnaise

⅓ cup honey

¼ cup lime juice

¼ tsp salt

In a small mixer bowl beat cream cheese at low speed until smooth, add remaining ingredients until well combined. Chill until ready to mix with chicken.

❀ ❀ ❀

Intelligent people have more zinc and copper in their hair.

Herb's Favorite Salad

1 head butter lettuce

1 can mandarin oranges

1 cup toasted pine nuts

1 cup Oriental dressing

Tear butter lettuce into small pieces and put in large salad bowl. Drain mandarin oranges well and add to lettuce, save leftover juice in small cup. Spread out pine nuts in a single layer on a cookie sheet and toast under oven broiler until light brown—watch carefully! Let cool and add to lettuce. Toss with dressing and serve.

Oriental Dressing

⅓ cup vinegar

¼ cup soy sauce

2 Tbs mandarin orange juice

1 tsp sesame oil

⅔ cup vegetable oil

Combine the first four ingredients in jar with tight-fitting lid and shake well. Add oil and shake again. Chill until ready to serve. Makes about 1½ cups.

❀ ❀ ❀

A comet's tail always points away from the sun.

Great and Tasty Chicken Section

I remember when I was real little, our traditional Sunday dinner was fried chicken and mashers, with lots of vegetables and sometimes a salad or slaw. Now chicken has become one of those great standby foods, great for casseroles, salads, or as the main course with vegetables. Also, you can substitute turkey for any chicken dish. Even though there are already chicken recipes in this cookbook, this section is devoted to some of the best recipes I've ever enjoyed. All righty then, here are some of the easiest ways to make great and tasty chicken.

❀ ❀ ❀

Too Easy Honey Chicken

This is an old standby that has been around in my family circle for as long as I can remember.

    1 chicken, cut into pieces, approximately 3 pounds

    ½ cup honey

    ½ cup prepared mustard

    2 Tbs butter

    Salt and pepper to taste

    Dash of paprika (optional)

Place chicken in a 9x13 glass casserole dish in a single layer. Melt butter, honey, and mustard (today that means that you zap the ingredients in the microwave). Add salt and pepper, stir until blended, then pour over the chicken. Sprinkle top with a dash of paprika. Do not cover. Bake in 325 degree oven for 1½ hours. (A little longer is fine if you need more time to...you know. Just cover lightly with aluminum foil and put the oven on warm for an extra 45 minutes. It won't hurt a thing.)

Now, I know what you're telling yourself, "It sounds too easy to really be super impressive," but trust me, the chicken is tender with a sweet and sour taste. Call it your "Special Secret Sauce" and refuse to divulge the family recipe.

❊ ❊ ❊

Rubber bands last longer when refrigerated.

Crock Pot Chicken

If you're going to take the "buns in bed" part of this cookbook seriously, then you must have a crock pot. There are lots of good ones. So you've gotten one within your budget and you're ready to begin. There are at least a million crock pot chicken recipes, so I'll include two I especially like. One of the best parts of crock pot cooking is the wonderful aroma that will fill the kitchen.

❀ ❀ ❀

Salsa Chicken

1 chicken, cut-up, cleaned, dried and rubbed with a little salt

1 jar salsa

Wash the chicken pieces and sprinkle with salt and pepper. Put in the crock pot and cover with salsa. Set crock pot on medium for first 3 hours. Check it occasionally to see if it needs any liquid. If it does, add a can of chicken broth. Then turn down to low for the next 5 hours. Serve when chicken is done. This is great served with tortilla chips and a salad.

❀ ❀ ❀

Remember that you are absolutely unique,
just like everyone else.

Spicy Chicken

Get out your trusty crock pot because it's going to be a long night.

    1 chicken, cut-up, cleaned and dried

    Cavender's® All Purpose Greek Seasoning

    ½ cup all-purpose flour

    ¼ cup vegetable oil

    ½ lb Italian sausage, hot or mild

    1 cup onion, chopped

    1 Tbs crushed hot peppers, fresh if possible

    1 Tbs garlic, chopped

    5 cans chicken broth

    ¼ cup green onions, chopped

Mix Greek seasoning and flour together in a bowl and put in chicken pieces until completely covered. Heat oil in cast iron skillet and brown your chicken pieces, about 6 minutes. Next add the onions and brown about 6 minutes. Take the sausage out of its casings, crumble up and add to the skillet, brown a few minutes more. Put in crock pot and add the hot peppers, garlic, and chicken broth. Cover the pot and let it simmer for 3 to 4 hours, until chicken is tender. Add the green onions and stir. Serve piping hot in a very pretty serving dish, with a good, crusty French or Italian bread for dipping in the broth.

❁ ❁ ❁

If you get into the bottom of a well or a tall chimney and look up, you can see stars, even in the middle of the day.

Stevie's Fat Chicken

Stevie Stanley is a dynamic girlfriend of mine. We share thoughts, ideas, and sometimes we just whine to each other, and yes, we have cheese with it.

1 Chicken
Seasoned salt to taste
Real Mayo
Corn Flakes

Preheat oven to 350 degrees.

Cut up chicken with the skin on, dry it and rub it with a little salt. Now rub the chicken pieces with real mayo and roll in crushed corn flakes. Put in 9x13 inch glass pan and bake at 350 degrees for 1 hour.

Serve with baked potatoes or mashers and a salad.

❁ ❁ ❁

The best thing to do behind a friend's back is to pat it.

Catalina Chicken

1 cut up chicken

1 bottle Catalina salad dressing

Marinate one cut-up chicken (about 3½ lbs.) in a bottle of Catalina salad dressing. An easy way to do this is to use a large plastic Ziplock® bag. I usually marinate this for at least 3 hours. Either put the chicken on the grill, basting it with the marinade, or bake it in a casserole dish, with some of the marinade poured over, in a 350 degree oven for about 1 hour. Save the extra marinade to serve with the chicken.

A variation of this recipe is to use a bottle of French dressing. Experiment and add some extra things that sound good to you like fresh mushrooms or other vegetables.

Also, you can do this chicken recipes in the crock pot as well. Just put in all the marinade and cook on low for at least 3 hours until chicken is done..

❀ ❀ ❀

A duck's quack doesn't echo and no one knows why.

Nellie's Lemon Garlic Chicken

Grandma Nellie loved green olives and garlic, so this is what she came up with for a chicken dish. The lemons give it extra zest. It's a little bit fancier than a lot of the recipes, but it really is tasty and colorful. Cousin Carole was able to track down some of Grandma Nellie's recipes when no one else could.

My favorite story is when Carole got Grandma Nellie's true homemade noodle recipe. Nellie would tell us how to make her noodles, but they turned out tough and hers were always tender. One day Carole walked in on Nellie as she was blanching the noodles in plain boiling water before putting them into the chicken broth. Nellie jumped a mile.

Carole said, "Nellie, you never told us about putting the noodles in plain boiling water first."

"Oh, I didn't?" Nellie said innocently. "I must have forgot."

> **3½ lbs. chicken pieces, you can use all legs and thighs if you want**
>
> **¼ cup chopped fresh mixed herbs (oregano, rosemary and thyme)**
>
> **2 Tbs chopped lemon rind**
>
> **⅓ cup fresh-squeezed lemon juice**
>
> **2 Tbs olive oil**
>
> **½ tsp salt**
>
> **¼ tsp pepper**
>
> **24 cloves of fresh garlic, peeled** (that's cloves, not bulbs)
>
> **1 cup chicken broth**
>
> **½ cup pitted green olives with pimento**
>
> **2 Tbs fresh chopped parsley**

Preheat oven to 425 degrees.

Mix herbs, lemon rind and juice, olive oil, salt and pepper together. Arrange chicken pieces in a roasting pan and spoon mixture over the pieces. Place garlic cloves around the chicken so the juice covers them. Bake at 425 degrees for 45 minutes. Remove from oven and gently transfer chicken and garlic onto serving dish. Add chicken broth to juice in the pan and stir. Add olives and heat through. Now pour this sauce over the chicken, sprinkle with fresh parsley and serve.

Note: When you buy or grow fresh herbs, once you've used them fresh, you can leave them on an open dish and let them dry. Then bag them and use when needed.

❀ ❀ ❀

Lemons are like a household tool. After you squeeze lemons, keep what's left by the sink and use them to remove other smells from your hands. Or you can stick them on your elbows while you are reading a book to soften and whiten your skin.

Carole's Chicken Casserole

This is one of my favorites from my Cousin Carole Pope. Her ability to combine ingredients into the most delicious casseroles is amazing. These one is definitely a comfort food recipe. It's easy and really good.

>   4 whole chicken breasts
>
>   8 oz noodles or spaghetti of your choice
>
>   2 cans cream of mushroom soup
>
>   2 cups shredded cheddar cheese
>
>   1 tsp crushed rosemary, plus a pinch
>
>   ½ lb fresh mushrooms, sliced (optional)
>
>   1 cup crumbled potato chips

Preheat oven to 350 degrees. Get out your favorite casserole dish that is 9x13 inches.

Boil four whole chicken breasts, save the juice (or use 4 or 5 cups of leftover roasted chicken). Take the chicken out of the pot and boil the noodles in the juice. Drain and save the broth. After the chicken is cooled, cut it into chunks. If you're using leftovers, just boil the noodles in regular water and add a can of chicken broth to the casserole later.

If you're using mushrooms, sauté them in a skillet in a little unsalted butter. Now put the two cans of cream of mushroom soup, shredded cheddar cheese, mushrooms and rosemary in the casserole dish, stir together well. Add the chicken and noodles and stir some more. Add the juice or chicken broth to make it creamy.

Cover with aluminum foil and bake for 30 minutes. Take out of oven and remove the foil, stir it again, then add the crumbled potato chips on top and bake for another 30 minutes, uncovered.

Important Note: Add no salt to this recipe.

This one is especially good if you are having a dinner party for your close friends. They will rave about your sweet, old-fashioned girl qualities, and your fella will chime in with the compliments.

❁ ❁ ❁

Life in abundance comes only through love! xx

Baked Chicken Breasts

This is a little different and very good.

    8 halved chicken breasts, boneless and skinless

    8 slices of bacon

    1 can cream of chicken soup

    1 soup can of water

    1 cup sour cream

    1 (2.5 oz) package dried beef

Preheat oven to 275 degrees.

Grease bottom of 9x13 inch glass baking pan, then line with dried beef. Wrap each chicken breast with a slice of bacon and lay on top of the dried beef. Mix soup, water and sour cream together and pour over the chicken. Bake at 275 degrees for 3 hours. This dish can be prepared a day ahead and refrigerated before baking.

❀ ❀ ❀

The tooth is the only part of the human body
that cannot heal itself.

Carole Pope's Cookie Section

My cousin, Carole, is one of the best cooks I know. She makes every meal special and always makes me feel welcome when I visit. I was 14 years old when she married Jess, who was like the older brother I never wanted. Through the years, I've always felt especially close to Carole. She has a kind, positive thought to share whenever we talk. This section is dedicated to Carole's cookies. They are wonderful, so enjoy!

❀ ❀ ❀

Pecan Snappers

These are super easy and very good.

1 German chocolate cake mix

2 eggs

⅔ cup butter or butter Crisco®

Pecan halves

Preheat oven to 350 degrees. Beat eggs, Crisco® and about half of the cake mix until smooth. Then, stir in the rest of the mix. Place three pecans, with ends touching in the center, on your cookie sheet. Shape dough into 1 inch balls and spread on the nuts.

Bake at 350 degrees for 10 minutes.

Browned Butter Icing

⅓ cup butter

about 2 Tbs milk

1½ tsp vanilla

3 cups powdered sugar

Heat butter in a saucepan over medium heat until it is a delicate brown color. Remove from heat and stir in the sugar, vanilla and milk. Beat until the frosting is smooth and is a spreading consistency. Use this on your Pecan Snappers, or any other iced cookie. You can cheat and use ready-made icing, but it won't be as good.

The quality of your life begins in your mind. xx

Carole's Famous Chocolate Chip Cookies

I believe these are the world's best chocolate chip cookies! And I have made them for countless people who agree.

Sift together, then set aside:

2¼ cups flour

1 tsp baking soda

1 tsp salt

Combine:

¾ cup butter Crisco®

¾ cup granulated sugar

¾ cup firmly packed brown sugar

1½ tsp pure vanilla

½ tsp water

Preheat oven to 375 degrees.

Beat the butter Crisco, sugar and brown sugar until really creamy! It is very important that you beat these items together until the batter is fluffy. Then, slightly beat 2 medium eggs It is important that you use medium eggs, not large, Now add eggs to mixture. Now be sure to beat until really creamy. The mixture will be a very light color and fluffy.

Slowly add in the flour mixture and mix well. Once this is done, you will be adding in the chocolate chips by hand. Stir in at least a 12 oz pack of chocolate chip. Remember, these are chocolate chip cookies ,so the more chocolate chips the better.

Bake at 375 degrees for 11 minutes. Remove from oven and put cookies on a rack until cooled.

For a sheet cookie, use a 9x13 pan, bake for 20 minutes, cut in squares, and serve. Oatmeal Cookies: Omit the chocolate chips and add 1½ cups of oats and 2 cups of coconut.

❀ ❀ ❀

"All you need is love. But a little chocolate now and then doesn't hurt."
Charles M. Schulz

Sugar Cookies

1 cup granulated sugar

1 cup butter, room temperature

2 eggs

3 Tbs milk

1 tsp baking soda

2 tsp vanilla

3 cups all-purpose flour

½ tsp salt

Preheat oven to 350 degrees. Cream the butter and sugar together and add the beaten eggs. Mix baking soda in the milk and add to mixture. Add flour, salt and vanilla. Refrigerate the dough for about an hour before rolling and cutting with a cookie cutter. Bake at 350 degrees for 10 minutes.

Icing:

1 lb powdered sugar

1 cup white Crisco®

2 tsp vanilla

1 egg white

Dash of salt

Add all ingredients together in the mixer and add a little milk, as needed, for a spreading consistency.

❀ ❀ ❀

Humans are born craving sugar.

Double Peanut Butter Cookies

3 cups flour

1 tsp baking soda

1 cup butter Crisco®

½ cup light corn syrup

1 cup granulated sugar

½ tsp salt

1 cup peanut butter (I like to use Peter Pan® Crunchy)

2 Tbs milk

Preheat oven to 350 degrees. Mix dry ingredients, cut in Crisco® and peanut butter until mixture resembles coarse meal. Blend in syrup and milk. Shape into 2 inch rolls and chill.

When you are ready to bake your cookies, slice the rolls into ¼ to ⅛ inch thick slices. Place one slice on ungreased cookie sheet, spread with about ½ tsp peanut butter, add top slice, seal edge with a fork. Gently sprinkle cookies with sugar.

Bake at 350 degrees for 12 minutes. Cool slightly before removing from cookie sheet.

❀ ❀ ❀

It's not old behavior if you're still doing it.

Salted Peanut Cookies

1 cup margarine

2 cups brown sugar

2 eggs, beaten

2 cups flour

½ tsp salt

1 tsp baking powder

1 tsp baking soda

1 cup Wheaties® cereal

2 cups quick-cooking rolled oats

1 cup chopped salted peanuts

Preheat oven to 375 degrees.

In a large mixing bowl with an electric mixer, beat margarine and brown sugar until fluffy, add eggs and blend together. Sift together flour, salt, baking powder and baking soda. Add to margarine mixture and mix well. Stir in cereal and oats, then stir in peanuts.

Drop by teaspoons onto lightly greased baking sheet. Press with fork to flatten.

Bake at 375 degrees for 11 minutes.

❄ ❄ ❄

I just got a call from my family—Cat, Leo, Jill, Jenny, John, and Madison. They said, "Let's go to Universal Studios® for the day," so I'm going. That's another reason why I live in Florida now.

Lemon Love 'Em Cookies

1 stick of butter room temperature

8 oz cream cheese room temperature

1 egg

1 Tbs lemon juice

1 box lemon cake mix

1 cup powdered sugar

Preheat oven to 350 degrees.

Cream butter and cream cheese together until creamy. Add egg and lemon juice Mix on low until combined. Add the lemon cake mix in three parts, mixing until combined after each part.

Refrigerate dough for 2 hours. Remove from fridge. Roll into 1 inch balls and roll through the powdered sugar. Place on cookie sheets covered with parchment paper.

Bake 10-12 minutes. Cool for two minutes and remove to cookie cooling racks. When fully cool dust with more powdered sugar.

❀ ❀ ❀

Your tongue is the only muscle in your body
that is attached at only one end.

Almond Crunch Cookies

1½ cups butter, softened

1 cup brown sugar

1 cup sugar

2 large eggs

2 tsp vanilla extract

2¼ cups all purpose flour

1 tsp baking power

⅛ tsp salt

1 cup finely chopped almonds

Preheat oven to 350 degrees.

Cream together butter and sugars, until light and fluffy, about 5 minutes. Add in eggs and vanilla and beat again. Combine flour, baking powder and salt. Add flour mixture to dough, one third at a time until all added. Stir in almonds.

Using a small cookie scoop, place dough on a parchment lined baking sheet three inches apart (these cookies spread.) Bake at 350 degrees for 8-9 minutes, until edges turn golden. Let cool on baking sheet for five minutes before removing to racks to cool completely.

❀ ❀ ❀

The microwave was invented in 1945 when a scientist, developing a radar transmitter, noticed that a candy bar in his pocket was melting.

Chocolate Fudge Cookies

2½ cups all purpose flour

1 cup cocoa

1¼ tsp baking soda

¼ tsp salt

1¼ cups unsalted butter (room temperature)

 2¼ cups sugar

3 eggs

2½ tsp vanilla

¼ cup sugar, set aside

Pre-heat the oven to 350°F.

Using an electric mixer, cream together the butter and sugar. Add the vanilla and combine. In a separate bowl combine the flour, baking soda, salt, and cocoa. Whisk to combine and set aside. Into the creamed butter/sugar mixture, beat in the eggs.

Pour the wet ingredients into the dry and combine using a mixing spoon.Form the dough into balls roughly the size of golf balls. Roll and coat them in the reserved ¼ sugar.

Place 6 balls evenly spaced onto a parchment paper lined cookie sheet and bake for about 12 minutes. Once the first 6 are done, then the next can go into the oven. Do not crowd cookies. It's a good idea to use 2 cookie sheets.

Allow the cookies to cool on cookie sheet for a 3 minutes before moving them onto a cooling rack.

❀ ❀ ❀

May your heart dance with the joy of each moment!

Pumpkin Spice Cookies

1 (18.25 oz) box spice cake mix
1 (15 oz) can solid pack pumpkin
12 oz chocolate chips
½ tsp pure vanilla extract
2 tsp sugar if needed

Preheat oven to 350 degrees. Grease cookie sheets and set aside.

In a large bowl, stir together cake mix, vanilla, and pumpkin until well blended. Drop by rounded spoonfuls onto the prepared cookie sheet. Bake for 18 to 20 minutes in the preheated oven. Allow cookies to cool on baking sheet for 5 minutes before removing to a wire rack to cool completely.

Vanilla Glaze:
1 cup powdered sugar
1 Tbs milk
½ tsp pure vanilla extract

Drizzle vanilla glaze over the cookies.

P.S. Carole has somehow managed to stay a perfect size six, even though she's baked millions of her cookies over the years.

❀ ❀ ❀

Inspiration is life reaching out to you and inviting you to dance.

Stuff for Your Own Good

This is a very short section on purpose. While these are great suggestions and they do work, you really can eat almost anything, so long as you do not overeat.

❀ ❀ ❀

Nan's Healthy Principles

Let me begin with a few healthy principles to live by:

1. Chew, chew, chew your food at least 20 times, something most of us have forgotten to do. No more wolfing down your food.

2. Drink no liquids with your meals. Use them 15 minutes before or after you eat. Otherwise you wash your food down without chewing it enough. Remember rule number one: chew, chew, chew.

3. Do a focused breathing exercise at least 10 minutes per day. Extra oxygen does wonders in your body.

4. Pay attention to food combining, unless it's a traditional occasion where certain foods are always served.

5. Eat when you're hungry, not starved. Stop when you're satisfied, not stuffed.

6. Eat smaller meals. (Now that's rocket science!)

7. Eat fresh, organic foods when possible.

8. Eat what your body wants right then; otherwise, the food will not satisfy you, and you will overeat.

9. Use glass cookware, or stainless steel, or cast iron; no more aluminum, period.

10. Oh, did I mention chewing? Well, chew some more!

❀ ❀ ❀

Why do people constantly return to the refrigerator with hopes that something new to eat will have materialized?

Theee Hooolidaaaays

These few simple ideas will make a huge difference in your overall health and the way your body digests food. And a very happy by-product will be a reduction in your body fat.

Let's be real. Unless you are a totally disciplined person, there will be times when overeating will just happen. It could be a family outing, a wedding, a birthday celebration or, of course, "theee hooolidaaaays." Whoever decided that we should eat boring food to be slender is full of crap. (Yes, I said crap in a cookbook, so just get over it.) I believe we need to be liberated, to have an entirely different attitude. Foods are fun and they taste good, so here's what to do:

1. Eat only when your stomach is hungry and you feel a hunger pang.

2. Eat only the most inviting foods—pass by anything that looks just so-so.

3. Eat enough food, but not too much food, about the size of your fist, three or four times a day.

4. Save room in your stomach for dessert, if you want dessert. Then, eat only a few bites, not the whole serving. If you are worried about the starving people in the world, put your leftovers in an envelope and mail it to them.

5. If there are more foods at a meal that you want to eat, but you know there is not enough room in your stomach, taste rather than eat the foods. Remember, if it tastes really good to you, you can most likely eat it again another day.

6. Savor every single bite and taste. Remember, chew, chew, chew.

7. Go easy on the alcohol. It contributes to weight gain and can also impair your ability to feel stomach hunger.

8. Make the event and the people more important than the food. Skinny people do this naturally.

9. If you have multiple parties to go to in one day, taste rather than eat at the parties.

10. Avoid talking about your weight loss program.

11. Maintain your exercise program throughout the holidays. An hour a day is ideal. A half hour is the minimum you need to feel great. Fifteen minutes is better than nothing. And if that doesn't work, just exercise for whatever amount of time you can. Pick whatever you like best and just do it!

12. Get out of doors for fresh air and sunshine once or twice a day (which is why I live in Florida, except on hurricane days).

13. Eat like there will be a tomorrow!

❀ ❀ ❀

Like fingerprints, everyone's tongue print is different.
(I wonder who discovered this.)

Food Combining Groups

Dense proteins such as meat, fish, dairy products, nuts, seeds, avocados and coconut are best combined with green vegetables, including spinach, celery, cucumbers, zucchini, peppers, sprouts and broccoli. Also, dense proteins work well combined with less dense starch and other foods such as tomatoes, root vegetables, beets, cabbage and cauliflower. It is best to not eat dense starches with dense proteins.

Dense starches include potatoes, grains, beans, peas, winter squash, corn and artichokes.

Dense starches are best eaten with green vegetables, including spinach, celery, cucumbers, zucchini, peppers, sprouts and broccoli. Also, dense starches work well combined with less dense starch and other foods such as tomatoes, root vegetables, beets, cabbage and cauliflower.

Green vegetables are also good combined with the less dense starch and other food group.

Here are some quick rules to remember about proper food combining:

1. Have liquids alone or liquids first, before other foods, and then wait at least 15 minutes. (Coffee is the exception, as I stated earlier.)

2. Do not combine dense proteins with dense starches.

3. Eat fruits alone, separate from your meal or other foods.

4. Eat melons alone.

Amount of time various foods stay in your stomach:

Water: 10-15 minutes

Juice: 15-30 minutes

Fruit: 30-60 minutes

Melons: 30-60 minutes

Most vegetables: 1-2 hours

Grains and Beans: 1-2 hours

Dense Vegetable Protein: 2-3 hours

Meat and Fish: 3-4 hours

Shellfish: 8 hours

There will be more delicious recipes to come in many more cookbooks. In the meantime, remember when you put your biscuits in the oven, make time to put your buns in bed!

❀ ❀ ❀

"Words are, of course, the most powerful drug used by mankind."
Rudyard Kipling

Acknowledgments

This cookbook has been a long time in the making, and it includes many recipes that have grown through generations. First and foremost, I want to thank my sister, Cathy (Cat) Spires, and my nieces, Jenny Rebecca (Jen) Jump and Jillian Reed (Jill) Spires, for their many contributions to give this cookbook extra excitement and appeal, to Jenny's husband, John, for being a good recipe taster, and to Little Madison, who calls me her great and beautiful Aunt Nan when she wants cookies. And Cat and Leo, thanks for always believing in me.

An enormous thank you to Cheryl Baraniak, who was my daily mentor and voice of encouragement in bringing this cookbook to the light. Thank you to Clancy Imislund, the master of one liners, some of which are included in this book.

A huge thank you to my "voice of reason," Carolyn Litwin, who had the job of keeping me focused and on track. Without you, Kid, I would not have been able to find the paper scraps that held the treasures included in this book. Also, I want to thank JoAnn Kalson-Vernon for editing the original digital edition of Put Your Biscuits in the Oven and Your Buns in Bed.

To all of you who have shared your recipes along the way, including Cousin Carole Pope, Tina Lewis, Sherrie Hill, Mildred Collins, and to Mom, Grandma Nellie, Grandma Grace, and Marie Harding, who left their recipes as part of our heritage, and other friends and family, thank you big.

Cooking is meant to be fun, creative, and shared. It's been a blast!

Nancy DeLong

Other Books by Nancy DeLong

Salmon In The Dishwasher
Always Wash Your Nuts
Let Go Or Be Dragged
Bouquets From God
I'm Just Sayin'
Happy Birthday Jesus
Ride The Wind
Reba Z
That's The Rule

…and oodles more to come

nancydelong.com

CPSIA information can be obtained
at www.ICGtesting.com
Printed in the USA
LVHW101244040819
626450LV00022B/1003/P